Essential Legal Documents

and

Funeral Pre-Planning Kit

Large Print Edition

Essential Legal Documents
and
Funeral Pre-Planning Kit

Large Print Edition

O. Chip Robinson

Wanderin Nomad Press
Because knowledge IS power.
PO Box 219, Smiths Station, AL 36877
wanderinnomadpress@gmail.com

<u>DISCLAIMER</u>

This book is not intended to be a replacement for legal advice. The author is not an attorney and in no way represents herself as one. The intended purpose of this book is to give everyone the tools needed to prepare basic legal documents and to make medical and funeral wishes known, easily accessible, and affordable.

You are encouraged to consult with an attorney as needed.

DEDICATION

This book, my first since you died, is dedicated to you, Mom. You spent 45 years of your long life as a nurse in one field or another. You cared for thousands of aged, sick, broken, and psychotic patients during your career. From Life Flight, trauma and emergency patients, maternity patients, injured soldiers on the battlefield in Vietnam. You name the setting; you have cared for them.

With every patient you encountered you showed them all love, respect, and compassion. Even the AIDS patient who intentionally stabbed you with the needle you had just used on him. But it was your work with hospice patients that you absolutely loved. You were an advocate for dying with dignity and assisted suicide before any medical care and legislation was ever in place.

I remember when you took Hospice education and training in 1984. You talked to my brother and I about the process of death, and the cycles of grief. You were so excited to have the opportunity to make sure the dying was comfortable and ready, and that death itself was not something to fear. It's the pain, the loneliness, and dying with regrets that we truly fear. Not death. Death is just a word for the end of our time.

Because of this, you were ready when your time came. We were ready. You always talked to us about your final wishes. When you were given the news that you were at the end of your life, the only thing left for us to do was reminisce and celebrate you and your amazing life. You made sure we knew you were proud of us. You made sure to say a final "I love you" and "goodbye" to those who mattered to you. Once you were ready you had your pain medication increased so you would fall asleep and go peacefully. And you did.

I am so grateful that you were completely coherent in your final days. I am so thankful that we were able to hear from you how much you loved us and why you were so proud of us. We know how lucky we were to have had that with you. Because of that, because of you, Mom, is why I have written this book. I want to show that the end of our lives can be an incredibly beautiful thing, when you plan for it.

Thank you, Mom. Thank you for teaching me how to be compassionate, and how to show empathy for others. Thank you for teaching me not to judge people, no matter their situation. When it comes to death, we are all going to experience it. Some will not get the chance to say goodbye, while others, like you, will have planned for it. When our time comes, our loved ones will be ready because we have pre-planned.

I love you, Mom!

Carol Linda Prater

September 16, 1947 – April 4, 2024

Finally, back on Dodi's Farm

Table of Contents

Introduction

Accidents, illness, and death are an inevitable part of our lives. Death is the only guarantee we all have. Unfortunately, we do not know the hour of our death or when an incapacitating event will occur. If we did, we would have plenty of time to prepare for it.

It is not just our healthcare and death for which we must prepare. Even if you are disabled, unable to perform a legal task for yourself because you are out of the area, or unavailable for some other reason, you should have someone with your best interest in mind ready to act on your behalf.

Unfortunately, many of us will leave our loved ones scrambling to plan and pay for our funeral. By not having the documents in place, or at the very least, having a conversation about our wishes, we leave our loved ones suffering during the most devastating and emotional times of their life. You can eliminate any added stress and lingering doubts about your medical care, belongings, and funeral plans by preparing in advance.

When it comes to our healthcare, belongings, and funeral we must have legal documents in place that will speak for us and eliminate any burden left for our loved ones to endure. These documents are crucial for everyone to have no matter your socioeconomic status. Fortunately, you can prepare these documents **yourself** at home, without the need for an attorney you may not be able to afford.

Talking about our mortality or major healthcare decisions is difficult for some people but using this "Do It Yourself" kit can make it an easier topic to discuss. There is no better time than the present to ensure your affairs are in order and prepare for what is to come.

The Power of Attorney

A Power of Attorney, or POA, is a document that is used to appoint someone you trust to legally act on your behalf if you become incapacitated or unable to perform a duty yourself. After careful consideration you, the principal, will designate another individual, the Agent, to act as your attorney-in-fact by laying out the specific duties you allow them to conduct on your behalf. This can be for a specified amount of time or permanent with no termination date.

A power of attorney can be revoked, or terminated, at any time in writing, or by appointing a new Agent. Once your Power of Attorney is completed you must sign it in front of a Notary Public who will verify your identity. The Notary Public stamp is what will make your document a legally binding document. Once you have completed a power of attorney you will want to make at least two copies. One will be given to your assigned Agent and the other you can put up for safekeeping. Additionally, you can take the original power of attorney to the Recorder of Deeds in your county and have it recorded for a small fee. This is a great option to make sure that there will always be a certified copy available should you lose any of the other copies.

There are many potential reasons for you to need a power of attorney. If you were to ever become mentally or physically unable to perform legal duties for yourself, you would want someone in place who can oversee your affairs for you. This is extremely important for anyone who is elderly, disabled, traveling out of the country, or is a member of the military. Or if you are facing a serious medical issue that may make it difficult or impossible to perform the duties yourself.

As an added layer of protection, you can specify in the power of attorney that it will not go into effect until a doctor certifies you as mentally incompetent. You may even name a specific doctor who you wish to determine your competency or require that two licensed physicians agree on your mental state.

No law in the United States requires an attorney to prepare your power of attorney for you. It does not require any specific formatting or length, and, by law, your self-prepared document is to be given the same legal effect as a power of attorney that has been prepared by a lawyer. You will, however, want to do some research and make sure to include any legal statements in your power of attorney that are legally required in your state. Not all states have these requirements but to protect yourself, please do your research.

The most important aspect of any power of attorney is to whom you are giving this power. Are they trustworthy? Are they capable of performing your duties? Will they act in your best interest? If you are confident that this individual can conduct your legal rights and will act in your best interest, you are ready to decide what powers you will grant them and for how long your power of attorney will be valid. You may even want to designate two individuals to be your agents who work together on your behalf. You will want to do some research to make sure to include any legal statements in your power of attorney that are required in your state. Not all states have these requirements but to protect yourself, do your research.

Furthermore, some states require that a power of attorney be recorded with the county courthouse. Be sure to call your local courthouse and ask if you will be required to do this.

There are many different powers of attorney. The type you need will be determined by what you need the document to do.

A **General Power of Attorney** will allow your assigned Agent to act as you, the Principal, in almost any legal situation, such as opening and closing bank accounts, handling financial transactions, buying life insurance, settling claims, operating your business, invoking or waiving contractual rights, registering your vehicle, buying and selling your property (personal and real), managing your real estate, and collecting debts owed to you. A General Power of Attorney is often used in estate planning to make sure someone is in place to manage your financial matters.

The General Power of Attorney does have some drawbacks to be aware of. While this type of power of attorney can be the easiest one to have, some institutions may not accept it. This is one reason that you must have the correct type of power of attorney based on your specific needs.

A **Special or Limited Power of Attorney** gives specific powers to your agent for a specific amount of time. You may allow your agent to only perform your financial, business, or medical duties for one certain day, or longer.

A **Military Power of Attorney** is used by members of the military who are on deployment or assigned to an unaccompanied tour. It will give the designated agent the power to take care of the service member's legal affairs while on deployment.

A **Springing Power of Attorney**, or conditional power of attorney, only goes into effect if a specific event or medical condition, typically incapacitation, occurs. It can end at a specified time when you become incapacitated upon death. For example, military personnel may draft a springing power of attorney that goes into effect when deployed overseas.

Durable or Nondurable

A **Durable Power of Attorney** is effective immediately after you sign it unless stated otherwise. It allows your agent to continue acting on your behalf if you become incapacitated. It will automatically terminate upon your death.

Table 1.1

Power of Attorney Sample Powers

This is a short example of the powers you can grant to your agent(s) in a power of attorney.

Automobiles

Real Property Transactions

Tangible Personal Property Transactions

Stock and Bond Transactions

Banking and Other Financial Institutions Transaction

Business Operating Transactions

Insurance and Annuity Transactions

Estate, Trust, and Other Beneficiary Transactions

Court Claims and Litigation

The Department of Veterans Affairs

Social Security Administration

The Department of Defense

The Department of the Army, Marines, Navy, etc.

Defense Enrollment Eligibility Reporting System (DEERS)

County and State Government Agencies

Retirement Plan Transactions

Tax Matters

A **Nondurable Power of Attorney** expires if you become incapacitated or die. For example, if you fall into a coma, your agent will lose the authority previously granted to act on your behalf. If that happens, only a court-appointed guardian or conservator will be able to make decisions for you, unless you have another

document in place granting your agent the
authority to act on your behalf.

Your Healthcare Documents

Advance care planning involves discussing and preparing for future decisions about your medical care if you become seriously ill or unable to communicate your wishes. Having meaningful conversations with your loved ones is the most important part of advance care planning. Many people choose to put their preferences in writing by completing legal documents called Advance Directives.

Advance directives are legal documents that provide instructions for your medical care and only go into effect if you cannot communicate your wishes. The two most common advance directives for healthcare are the Living Will and the Healthcare Power of Attorney.

Advance care planning is not just for people who are old or ill. At any age, a medical crisis could leave you unable to communicate your healthcare decisions. Planning now for your future health care can help ensure you get the medical care you want and that someone you trust will be there to make decisions for you.

If you do not have an advance directive and you are unable to make decisions on your own, the state laws where you live will determine who may make medical decisions on your behalf. This is typically your spouse, your parents if they are available, or your children if they are adults.

If you are unmarried and have not named your partner as your healthcare proxy, it's possible they could be excluded from decision-making. If you have no family members, some states allow a close friend who is familiar with your values to help. Or they may assign a physician to represent your best interests.

Even though an advance directive is a

Table 1.2

Alzheimer's Disease

Many people do not realize that Alzheimer's disease and related dementias are terminal conditions and ultimately result in death. People in the later stages of dementia often lose their ability to do the simplest tasks. If you have dementia, advance care planning can give you a sense of control over an uncertain future and enable you to participate directly in decision-making about your future care.

If you are a loved one of someone with dementia, encourage these discussions as early as possible. In the later stages of dementia, you may wish to discuss decisions with other family members, your loved one's healthcare provider, or a trusted friend to feel more supported when deciding the types of care and treatments your loved one may want.

legally recognized document, it may not be legally binding. This means that your healthcare provider and proxy will do their best to respect your advance directives, but there may be circumstances when they cannot exactly follow your wishes. For example, you may be in a complex medical situation where it is unclear what you would want. Or there is a possibility that a healthcare provider refuses to follow your advance directives. This can be because the decision goes against the healthcare provider's conscience, the healthcare institution's policy, or accepted healthcare standards.

If a situation like this arises, the healthcare provider must inform your healthcare proxy immediately and consider transferring you to another healthcare provider or facility.

A **Living Will** is a document that tells your doctors and family what medical treatments you do and do not want to be used to keep you alive and your wishes regarding pain management and organ donation.

When determining your wishes and the life-saving measures you want, if there is ever a chance that you could be put on life support, think about your values. Consider how important it is to be independent and self-sufficient then identify what circumstances might make you feel like your life is not worth living. Would you want treatment to extend your life in any situation? All situations? Would you want treatment only if a cure is possible?

To ensure your wishes are followed, you can have your doctor complete a Do Not Resuscitate (DNR) and Do Not Intubate (DNI) order to be added to your medical file. Even if you already have a living will that includes your preferences regarding resuscitation and intubation, it is still a good idea to complete do not resuscitate and or do not intubate orders each time you are admitted to a new hospital or health care facility.

The **Healthcare Power of Attorney** grants your agent authority to make medical decisions for you if you are unconscious, mentally incompetent, or unable to make decisions on your own. The person you choose is called the healthcare agent, proxy, or surrogate. They are legally bound to act in your best interest.

The healthcare power of attorney can include instructions about the types of medical treatment you want, medication, surgery, and end-of-life care. It can also cover decisions about which doctors or facilities to use, what tests to run, and how aggressively to treat any medical conditions you may experience.

The healthcare power of attorney can help avoid situations where loved ones may not remember your wishes or instructions, they may interpret them differently than you intended or make decisions based on their own religious or moral beliefs.

The healthcare power of attorney is often combined with a durable power of attorney to protect the healthcare power of attorney if you lose the ability to make your own decisions. You can revoke or limit the healthcare power of attorney at any time.

For the healthcare power of attorney to be a legally binding document you must be at least 18 years of age and mentally competent when you sign the document. Additionally, the healthcare power of attorney may need to be signed by two witnesses who are not your spouse, relative, heir, beneficiary, or responsible for the cost of your medical care. In some states, you may be required to have your document signed by a Notary Public.

Some people spend a lot of time in more than one state. If that's your situation, consider preparing advance directives using the form for each state, and keep a copy in each place.

Once you have your advance directives in place you should review them at least once each year and update them if you've experienced any major life-changing events such as retirement, moving out of state, divorce or marriage, or if you have a significant change in your health.

What happens if you do not have an advance directive?

If you do not have an advance directive and you are unable to make decisions on your own, the state laws where you live will determine who may make medical decisions on your behalf. This is typically your spouse, your parents if they are available, or your children if they are adults. If you are unmarried and have not named your partner as your proxy, it's possible they could be excluded from decision-making. If you have no family members, some states allow a close friend who is familiar with your values to help. Or they may assign a physician to represent your best interests. To find out the laws in your state, contact your state legal aid office or state bar association.

<table>
<tr><td>

Table 1.3

Medical Care Options

There are several end-of-life care decisions to consider when drafting your living will. If you have questions about any of the following medical decisions, please consult with your physician.

- Cardiopulmonary resuscitation (CPR) restarts the heart when it has stopped beating.

- Mechanical ventilation takes over breathing if you're unable to breathe on your own.

- Tube feeding supplies the body with nutrients and fluids intravenously or via a tube in the stomach.

- Dialysis removes waste from your blood and manages fluid levels if your kidneys no longer function.

- Antibiotics or antiviral medications can be used to treat many infections.

- Comfort care (palliative care) includes any number of interventions that may be used to keep you comfortable and manage pain while abiding by your other treatment wishes.

- Organ and tissue donations for transplantation can be specified in your living will. If your organs are removed for donation, you will be kept on life-sustaining treatment temporarily until the procedure is complete.

- Donating your body for scientific study also can be specified. Contact a local medical school, university, or donation program for information on how to register for a planned donation for research.

</td></tr>
</table>

THIS PAGE INTENTIONALLY LEFT BLANK

- 24 -

POWER OF ATTORNEY
Templates

DURABLE POWER OF ATTORNEY

(Comprehensive Sample)

KNOWN ALL MEN BY THESE PRESENT, that I
_____________________, date of birth
_____________________, last four of Social Security
Number ______, hereinafter referred to as the
"Principal", do hereby designate and appoint
_____________________, date of birth
_____________________, last four of Social Security
Number ______, hereinafter referred to as the
"Agent", as my true and attorney in fact, to have
full power and authority to:

1. **Automobiles**. To use, operate, license,
register, insure, purchase, or sell any vehicles of
which I am the registered or legal owner.

2. **Real property** transactions. To lease, sell,
mortgage, purchase, exchange and acquire, and
to agree, bargain, and contract for lease, sale,
purchase, exchange, and acquisition of, and to
accept, take, receive, and possess any interest
in real property whatsoever, on such terms and
conditions, and under such covenants, as my
Agent shall deep proper, and to maintain, repair,

tear down, alter, rebuild, improve, manage, issue, move, rent, lease, sell, convey, subject to liens, mortgages, and security deeds, and in any way or manner deal with all or any part of any of my property lying in or being situated in any State within in the United States of America or any of the territories under United States ownership, under such terms and conditions and such covenants, as my Agent shall deem proper and may for all deferred payments accept purchase money notes payable to me and secured by mortgages or deeds to secure debt, and may from time to time collect and cancel any said notes, mortgages, security interests, or deeds to secure debt.

3. **Tangible personal property** transactions. To lease, sell, mortgage, purchase, exchange, acquire, and to agree, bargain, and contract for lease, sale, purchase, exchange, and acquisition of, and to accept, take, receive, and possess any personal property whatsoever, tangible or intangible, or interests in said property which are recognized by any State within the United States of America or its territories, and in any manner dealing with all or any part of real or personal property whatsoever, tangible or intangible, or any interest therein, that I own at the time of execution or may hereafter acquire,

under such terms and such covenants, as my Agent shall deem proper.

4.   **Stock and bond** transactions. To purchase, sell, exchange, surrender, assign, redeem, vote at any meeting, or otherwise transfer any shares of stock, bonds, or other securities in any business, association, corporation, partnership, or other legal entity, whether private or public, now or hereafter belonging to me.

5.   **Banking and other financial institution** transactions. To make, receive, sign, endorse, execute, acknowledge, deliver, and possess checks, drafts, bills of exchange, letters of credit, notes, stock certificates, withdrawal receipts, and deposit instruments relating to accounts or deposits in, or certificates of deposit of banks, savings and loans, credit unions, or other financial institutions or associations. To pay all sums of money, at any time or times, that may hereafter be owed by me upon any account, bill of exchange, check, draft, purchase, contract, note, or trade acceptance made, executed, endorsed, accepted, and delivered by me or for me in my name, by my Agent. To borrow from time to time such sums of money as my Agent may deem proper and execute promissory notes, security deeds or agreements, financing statements, or other security

instruments from time to time in whole or in part. To have free access to any time or times to any safe deposit box or vault to which I might have access.

6. **Business operating** transactions. To conduct, engage in, and otherwise transact the affairs of any lawful business ventures of whatever nature or kind that I may now or hereafter be involved in. To organize or continue and conduct any business which terms include, with or without limitation, any farming, manufacturing, mining, retailing, or other types of business operation in any form, whether sole proprietorship, joint venture, partnership, corporation, trust or other legal entity; operate, buy, sell, expand, contract, terminate or liquidate any business; direct, control, supervise, manage or participate in the operation of any business and exchange, compensate and discharge business managers, employees, agents, attorneys, accountants and consultants; and, in general, exercise all powers concerning business interests and operations which the principal could if present and under no disability.

7. **Insurance and annuity** transactions. To exercise or perform any act, power, duty, right, or obligation, regarding any contract of life,

accident, health, disability, liability, Medicare, Medicaid, or any other type of insurance or any combination of insurance; and to procure new or additional contracts of insurance for me and to designate the beneficiary of same; provided, however, that my Agent cannot designate himself or herself as beneficiary of any such insurance contracts.

8. **Estate, trust, and other beneficiary** transactions. To accept a receipt for, exercise, reject, renounce, assign, disclaim, demand, sue for, claim, and recover any legacy, bequest, devise, gift, or other property interest or payment due or payable to or for the principal; assert any interest in and exercise any power over any trust, estate or property subject to fiduciary control; establish a revocable trust solely for the benefit of the principal that terminates at the death of the principal and is then distributable to the legal representatives of the estate of the principal; and, in general, exercise all powers concerning estates and trusts which the principal could exercise if present and under no disability; provided, however, that the Agent may not make or change a will and may not revoke or amend a trust revocable or amendable by the principal or require the trustee of any trust for the benefit of the principal to pay income or principal to the

Agent unless specific authority to that end is given.

9. **Claims and litigation**. To commence, prosecute, discontinue, or defend all actions or other legal proceedings regarding my property, real or personal, or any part thereof, or touching any matter in which I or my property, real or personal, in any way concerned. To defend, settle, adjust, make allowances, compound, and demands whatsoever that now are, or hereafter shall be, pending between me and any person, firm, corporation, or other legal entity, in such manner and all respects as my Agent shall deem proper.

10. **Benefits** from the Department of Veterans Affairs, Social Security Administration, Department of Defense, Department of the Army, Marines, Navy, Air Force, Coast Guard, Space Force, Medicare, Medicaid, or other state or federal governmental programs, or military service. To prepare, sign, and file any claim or application for services and/or benefits; sue for, settle, or abandon any claim to benefit or assistance under any federal, state, local, or foreign statute or regulation; control, deposit to any account, collect receipt for, and take title to and hold all benefits under any Department of Veterans Affairs, Social Security Administration,

Department of Defense, Department of the Army, Medicare, Medicaid, or other governmental programs, or military service or other state, federal, local and foreign statute or regulation; and, in general, exercise all powers concerning any Department of Veterans Affairs, Social Security Administration, Department of Defense, Department of the Army, Medicare, Medicaid, or other governmental programs, or military service or other state, federal, local and foreign statute or regulation, which the principal could exercise if present and under no disability.

11. **Retirement plan** transactions. To contribute to, withdraw from, and deposit funds into any type of retirement plan (which term includes, without limitation, any tax-qualified or nonqualified pension, profit-sharing, stock bonus, employee savings and other retirement plans, individual retirement account, deferred compensation plan and any other type of employee benefit plan); select and change payment options for the principal under any retirement plan; make rollover contributions from any retirement plan to other retirement plans or individual retirement accounts; exercise all investment powers available under any type of self-directed retirement plan; and, in general, exercise all powers concerning retirement plans and retirement plan account

balances which the principal could if present and under no disability.

12. **Tax matters**. To prepare, to make elections, to execute and to file all forms relating to the Internal Revenue Service, any state, local, and foreign taxation service which the Agent shall deem necessary for safeguarding principal against excess or illegal taxation or penalties imposed for claimed violation of any law or other government regulation; and to pay, to compromise, or to contest or to apply for refunds in connection with any taxes or assessments for which principal may or may not be liable.

Limitation of Authority

The powers of the Agent herein shall be limited to the extent set out in writing in this durable power of attorney and shall not include the power to revoke or invalidate any previously existing declaration.

Effective Time

This durable power of attorney shall become effective immediately and shall not be affected by my subsequent disability or incapacity or upon the occurrence of my disability or incapacity.

Revocation

Any durable power of attorney I have previously made is hereby revoked.

This durable power of attorney shall only be revoked by an instrument in writing, executed, witnessed, or acknowledged in the same manner as required herein. This power of attorney shall not be affected by disability of the principal and shall continue to be effective should the principal become disabled, incompetent, or incapacitated.

Execution

This document was hereby executed on this _______ day of _________________, 20____ by:

____

Principal Signature

Acknowledgment

The above-named principal, personally known or acknowledged before me, this _______ day of _____________, 20____ in the State of _____________, County of _________________

______________________________   ______________________________

Notary Signature   Notary
Seal

My commission expires ___________

- 35 -

THIS PAGE INTENTIONALLY LEFT BLANK

SPECIAL MILITARY POWER OF ATTORNEY

(Comprehensive Sample)

THIS IS A MILITARY POWER OF ATTORNEY PREPARED AND EXECUTED UNDER TITLE 10, UNITED STATES CODE, SECTION 1044B, BY A PERSON AUTHORIZED TO RECEIVE LEGAL ASSISTANCE FROM THE MILITARY SERVICES. FEDERAL LAW EXEMPTS A MILITARY POWER OF ATTORNEY FROM ANY REQUIREMENT OF FORMS, SUBSTANCE, FORMALITY OR RECORDING THAT IS PRESCRIBED FOR POWERS OF ATTORNEY BY THE LAWS OF ANY STATE, COMMONWEALTH, TERRITORY, DISTRICT OR POSSESSION OF THE UNITED STATES, FEDERAL LAW SPECIFIES THAT A MILITARY POWER OF ATTORNEY SHALL BE GIVEN THE SAME LEGAL EFFECT AS A POWER OF ATTORNEY PREPARED AND EXECUTED UNDER THE LAWS OF THE JURISDICTION WHERE IT IS PRESENTED.

KNOWN TO ALL PERSONS that I, _________________, Department of Defense

Identification Number (DOD ID) ________________, a Service Member in the United States ________________ assigned to ________________, do hereby execute this SPECIAL MILITARY POWER OF ATTORNEY and do hereby appoint ________________, Department of Defense Identification Number (DOD ID) ________________ as my Attorney-in-Fact to act as follows, granting unto said Attorney the full power to:

1. **Automobiles**. To use, operate, insure, license, and register with any state or government agency, any vehicles I am presently the registered legal owner. To execute and deliver to the proper persons and authority any documents, instruments, and papers necessary to effect proper registration of any automobile in which I now or may hereafter have an interest in, or the sale thereof and transfer of legal title thereto as required by law, and to collect any receipt for all monies paid in consideration of such sale and/or transfer.

2. **Disposition of Property**. To sell, assign, transfer, exchange, convey, deed, mortgage, pledge, lease, let, license, demise, remise, quitclaim, bargain or otherwise dispose of any of my real estate, stocks, bonds, evidence of indebtedness and other

securities and other personal tangible and intangible or mixed property, or any custody, possession, interest or therein at public or private sale, upon such items, consideration, and conditions as my said attorney shall deem advisable and to execute, acknowledge and deliver such instruments and writings of whatsoever kind and nature as may be necessary, convenient or proper in the premises.

3. **Collection of Debts**.   To demand, collect, recover, sue for, receive, and give a receipt or release for any monies, debts, dividends, interests, royalties, legacies, annuities, demands, discounts, income, rents, profits, securities or other property of any sort, now or hereafter due or becoming due to me or to which I may be or hereafter become entitled.

4. **Endorsements**. A) to endorse and negotiate for any purpose all promissory notes, bills of exchange, checks, drafts, or other negotiable or non-negotiable paper payable to me or my order; B) To endorse for transfer all certificates of stock, bond, or other securities; C) To endorse and cash United States Savings Bonds and notes.

5. **Executing Government Vouchers**.   To execute vouchers on my behalf for any

allowances, compensation, and reimbursements properly payable to me by the Government of the United States or any agency or department thereof.

6. **Depositing Money and Other Property**. To deposit in my attorney's name or my name, or jointly in both our names, in any banking institution, funds, or property, and to withdraw any part of all my deposits at any time made by me on my behalf.

7. **Borrowing Money**. To borrow money in my name when deemed necessary to my said attorney upon such terms as to my said attorney appear proper and to execute such instruments as may be requisite for such purpose.

8. **Acquisition of Property**. To buy, receive, lease, accept, or otherwise acquire in my name and for my account property, real personal or mixed, upon such terms, considerations, and conditions as my said attorney shall deem proper.

9. **Recovering Possession of Property**. To eject, remove, or relieve tenants or other persons from, and recover possession of, any property, real, personal, or mixed in which I know or hereafter may have an interest.

10. **Litigation**.   To institute, maintain, defend, compromise, arbitrate, or otherwise dispose of, any actions, suits, attachments, or other legal proceedings for or against me, to the extent that such litigation is allowed.

11. **Tax Returns**.   To prepare and execute any tax returns, including, but not limited to, Federal Income Tax returns, State Income Tax returns, Social Security Tax returns, and Federal and State information and estimate returns; To execute and claims for funds, protests, applications for abatement, petitions to the United States Board of Tax Appeals or any other Board or Court, Federal or State, Consents and waivers to determination and assessment of taxes and consents and waivers agreeing to a later determination and assessment of taxes that is provided by statute of limitations; To receive and endorse and collect any checks in settlement of any refund of taxes; To examine and to request and receive copies of any tax returns, reports and other information from the United States Treasury Department or any other taxing authority, Federal or State, in connection with any of the foregoing matters.

12.   **Financial Institutions**.   To make deposits, withdrawals, and account inquiries regarding any checking or savings account with which I may hold an interest.

13.   **Defense Enrollment Eligibility Reporting System (DEERS)**. To enroll, change, or remove legal dependents in the Dependents Eligibility Enrollment Records System.

14.   **Army Emergency Relief (AER) (or other military branch)** To apply for, secure, receive, accept, and authorize repayment of any Army Emergency Relief loan or grant. Furthermore, to authorize the start or stop of any allotment associated with this action.

15.   **ID Cards**. To apply for or replace Dependent Identification Cards issued by the Department of Defense for my legal dependents as defined by applicable Military Branch or Department of Defense regulations, instructions, or directives.

16.   **Defense Finance and Accounting System (DFAS)**. To submit and receive information regarding pay inquiries, to start, stop, or change allotments; To receive copies of my Leave and Earning Statement(s) (LES).

17.   **Military Quarters**. To apply for, accept and terminate residence in military

quarters; To effect the assignments or termination of U.S. Government or other quarters, to sign for quarters, arrange for final inspection and clear quarters, and accept responsibility for the property therein; To sign in my name, place and stead any document whatsoever necessary under the law to accomplish the above-listed powers, and to make, sign, endorse, act, receive or accept any instrument of any kind or nature as may be necessary or proper to accomplish any of the above-said powers; Furthermore, to authorize the start or stop of any allotment associated with this action.

18. **Joint Personal Property Shipping Office (JPPSO)**. To ship, store, receive, and take possession of any personal, household property and goods, and personal vehicles through the Joint Personnel Property Shipping Office; To submit and receive any necessary claim for damages on any property.

19. **Dependent(s)**. To have care, custody, and control over my child/ren, _________________________ to authorize, enroll, and order all necessary items and services for my child's welfare and benefit, including but not limited to Exceptional Family Member Program (EFMP), Tricare, medical,

dental, pharmacy and surgical care, to create a Family Care Plan, schooling, clothing, housing, food and other necessities of life.

THIS SPECIAL MILITARY POWER OF ATTORNEY SHALL NOT BE AFFECTED BY DISABILITY OF THE PRINCIPLE AND SHALL CONTINUE TO BE EFFECTIVE SHOULD I BECOME DISABLED, INCOMPETENT OR INCAPACITATED BEFORE THE BELOW-STATED EXPIRATION DATE.

I HEREBY DECLARE THAT IF I SHALL BE REPORTED AS "MISSING" OR "MISSING IN ACTION" OR AS A "PRISONER OF WAR" AS THOSE PHRASES ARE USED IN MILITARY PARLANCE, SUCH DESIGNATION SHALL NOT BAR MY ATTORNEY-IN-FACT FROM FULLY AND COMPLETELY EXERCISING AND CONTINUING TO EXERCISE ANY AND ALL POWERS GRANTED HEREUNDER, AND THAT SUCH REPORT OR LISTING SHALL NEITHER CONSTITUTE NOR BE INTERPRETED AS CONSTITUTING NOTICE OF MY DEATH NOR SHALL IT OPERATE TO REVOKE THIS INSTRUMENT.

FURTHERMORE, I do hereby authorize my aforesaid attorney-in-fact to execute, acknowledge, and deliver any instrument under seal or otherwise, and to do all things necessary to carry out the intent hereof, hereby granting unto said attorney full power and authority to act in and concerning the premises as fully and effectually as I may do if personally present. Provided, however, that all business transacted hereunder for me, or my account shall be transacted in my name, and that all endorsements and instruments executed by my said attorney to carry out the foregoing powers shall contain my name, followed by that of my said attorney and the designation "attorney-in-fact".

TERMINATION I hereby declare that unless sooner terminated by me, and except as provided below, all powers granted herein to my attorney-in-fact shall terminate and this Special Military Power of Attorney shall become null and void on the _______ day of ____________________, 20___.

Notwithstanding my insertion of a specific expiration date herein, if on the above-specified expiration date, I shall be, or have been, carried in a military status of "missing", "missing in action", or "prisoner of war", then this power of attorney shall automatically remain valid and in full effect until sixty (60) days after I have returned to United States military control following the termination of such status.

IN WITNESS WHEREOF, I have hereunto set my hand and seal this _______ day of __________________, 20____.

____

Service Member Signature

_____________________________   _______________

Notary Signature   Notary Seal

My commission expires ____________

THIS PAGE INTENTIONALLY LEFT BLANK

HEALTHCARE POWER OF ATTORNEY and LIVING WILL

(Combined Sample)

I, ______________________________, state that this is my **Healthcare Power of Attorney**, and I revoke any prior Healthcare Power of Attorney signed by me. I understand the nature and purpose of this document. If any provision is found to be invalid or unenforceable, it will not affect the rest of this document.

This **Healthcare Power of Attorney** is in effect only when I cannot make healthcare decisions. However, this does not require or imply that a court must declare me incompetent.

I name ______________________________ to act as my healthcare agent or proxy, who will make healthcare decisions for me as authorized in this document.

If my named agent is unable or unwilling to serve, I name ______________________________ as my alternate healthcare agent or proxy, who will then make healthcare decisions for me as authorized in this document.

Any person can rely on a statement by any agent named above that he or she is properly acting under this document, and such a person does not have to make any further investigation or inquiry.

Guidance to Agent. My agent will make healthcare decisions for me based on the instructions that I have given in this or another document and on my wishes otherwise known to my agent. If my agent believes that my wishes as made known to my agent conflict with what is in this document, this document will control. If my wishes are unclear, my agent will make healthcare decisions in my best interests. My agent will determine my best interests after considering the benefits, the burdens, and the risks that might result from a given decision. If no agent is available, this document will guide decisions about my healthcare.

Authority of Agent. My agent has complete authority to make all healthcare decisions for me whenever I cannot make such decisions unless I have otherwise indicated below. This authority includes, but is not limited to, the following:

1. To consent to the administration of pain-relieving drugs, treatment, or procedures (including surgery) that my agent, upon medical

advice, believes may provide comfort to me, even though such drugs, treatment, or procedures may hasten my death. My comfort and freedom from pain are important to me and should be protected by my agent and physician.

2.   If I am in a terminal condition, to give, withdraw, or refuse to give informed consent to life-sustaining treatment, including artificially or technologically supplied nutrition or hydration.

3.   To give, withdraw, or refuse to give informed consent to any healthcare procedure, treatment, intervention, or other measure.

4.   To request, review, and receive any information, verbal or written, regarding my physical or mental health, including, but not limited to, all my medical and healthcare records.

5.   To consent to further disclosure of information, and to disclose medical and related information concerning my condition and treatment to other persons.

6.   To execute for me any releases or other documents that may be required to obtain medical and related information.

7.   To execute consents, waivers, and releases of liability for me and my estate to all persons

who comply with my agent's instructions and decisions. To indemnify and hold harmless, at my expense, any third party who acts under this Healthcare Power of Attorney. I will be bound by such indemnity entered by my agent.

8. To select, employ, and discharge healthcare personnel and services providing home health care and the like.

9. To select, contract for my admission, transfer, or authorize my discharge for any medical or healthcare facility, including, but not limited to, hospitals, nursing homes, assisted living facilities, hospices, adult homes, and the like.

10. To transport me or arrange for my transportation to a place where this Healthcare Power of Attorney is honored, should I become unable to make healthcare decisions for myself in a place where this document is not enforced.

11. To complete and sign for me the following: (Circle and initial your choice(s))

    a. Consents to health care treatment, or the issuance of Do Not Resuscitate (DNR) Orders or other similar orders; and

    b. Requests for my transfer to another facility, to be discharged against healthcare advice, or other similar requests; and

c. Any other document desirable to implement healthcare decisions that my agent is authorized to make under this document.

Special Instructions. By placing my initials at number three (3) below, I want to SPECIFICALLY AUTHORIZE MY AGENT TO REFUSE, OR IF TREATMENT HAS COMMENCED, TO WITHDRAW CONSENT TO, THE PROVISIONS OF ARTIFICIAL OR TECHNOLOGICALLY SUPPLIED NUTRITION OR HYDRATION IF: (Circle and initial your choice(s))

1. I am in a permanently unconscious state; and

2. My physician and at least one other physician who has examined me have determined, to a reasonable degree of medical certainty, that artificially or technologically supplied nutrition, and hydration will not provide comfort to me or relieve my pain; and

3. I have placed my initials on this line: _______

Limitations of Agent's Authority. I understand that some state laws require the following limitations to the authority of my agent:

1.   My agent cannot order the withdrawal of life-sustaining treatment unless I am in a terminal conditional or a permanently unconscious state, and two physicians have confirmed the diagnosis and have determined that I have no reasonable possibility of regaining the ability to make decisions; and

2.   My agent cannot order the withdrawal of any treatment given to provide comfort care or to relieve pain; and

3.   My agent cannot order the withdrawal of artificially or technologically supplied nutrition or hydration unless I am terminally ill or permanently unconscious and two physicians agree that nutrition or hydration will no longer provide comfort or relieve pain and, if I am permanently unconscious, I have given a specific direction to withdraw nutrition or hydration elsewhere in this document; and

4.   If I previously consented to any healthcare, my agent cannot withdraw that treatment unless my condition has significantly changed so that the healthcare is significantly less beneficial to me, or unless the healthcare is no longer significantly effective in achieving the purpose for which I chose the healthcare.

No Expiration Date. This Healthcare Power of Attorney will have no expiration date and will not be affected by my disability or the passage of time.

Guardian. I intend that the authority given to my agent will eliminate the need for any court to appoint a guardian of my person. However, should such proceedings start, I nominate my agent to serve as the guardian of my person, without bond.

Enforcement by Agent. My agent may take for me, at my expense, any action my agent considers advisable to enforce my wishes under this document.

Release of Agent's Personal Liability. My agent will not incur any personal liability to me or my estate for making reasonable choices in good faith concerning my health care.

Copies the Same as Original. Any person may rely on a copy of this document.

Out of State Application. I intend this document to be honored in any jurisdiction to the extent allowed by law.

Living Will. I do / do not have a Living Will. My wishes are stated within this Healthcare Power of Attorney and my designated agents are aware of my medical wishes.

Anatomical Gift. I do / do not hereby consent to organ and tissue donation, and I have made my wishes known regarding organ and tissue donation.

Donor Registry Enrollment Form. I have / have not completed the Donor Registry Enrollment.

Execution. I understand the purpose and effect of this document and hereby sign my name to this Healthcare Power of Attorney on this ____ day of __________________, 20___ by:

____

Principal Signature

Acknowledgment

The above-named principle is personally known or acknowledged before me this ___ day of __________________, 20___ in the State of __________________, County of ______________.

_______________________________   _______________________________

Notary Signature   Notary Seal

My commission expires _______________

- 56 -

THIS PAGE INTENTIONALLY LEFT BLANK

It's Your Funeral, Why Don't You Plan It?

Funeral Directors across America strongly encourage everyone to pre-plan or even pre-arrange their funeral. By doing this for yourself you will allow your loved ones to grieve without the added stress of planning your funeral. One of the hardest things families go through when making funeral arrangements is trying to pick what momma would have wanted or what daddy would have liked.

By pre-planning your funeral there is a record of what you want, particularly when it comes to cremation. States have different requirements when it comes to who could approve to have you cremated if you wanted it and didn't put it in writing.

In the State of Louisiana, for example, if you are not married when you die the state requires the majority of your next of kin to agree to a cremation before it can take place. Therefore, if you die and leave five adult children three of the five adult children must agree to your cremation. If they do not agree you will be buried. The only way around this potential problem is for you to authorize your cremation through self-authorization with pre-planning."

By pre-planning your funeral, you are making it easier for your family while making your funeral truly yours so when the time does come, there is very little left for your family to do.

Funerals today have become more personalized. Depending on the amount of money you want to spend, you have a plethora of options allowing you to pick out your style, color, or material of the casket or urn. You can pick up a catalog from any funeral home or search products online to decide for yourself what you want your earthly remains to spend the rest of eternity in.

Pre-planning does not require you to plan your funeral through a funeral director. It is as simple as documenting what you want to be done and storing it in a safe place where your next of kin can easily find it or give it to them to have when the time comes.

Later in this book is a funeral pre-planning guide, and some forms are readily available for download online. You can document whether you want a funeral or memorial service and the details. You can name who you want to deliver the eulogy, what music is to be played, and where you want your funeral held. When you pre-plan your funeral, you decide on those details.

Each year, Americans spend an estimated $20 billion on funeral services with the average traditional funeral costing $8,000-$10,000. The funeral industry is a service industry, and they are constantly changing to meet the needs of their clients while trying to maintain some traditional services.

One last topic to consider before we dive into funeral pre-planning is organ and tissue donation. If you are not already an organ donor, I strongly recommend that you consider becoming one. Organ and tissue donations save the lives of thousands of people every year, making it the ultimate gift anyone can give.

If you become a donor, once you die, or declared brain dead, your organs will be harvested and transported into either a recipient for transplant, or to a tissue bank where it will be processed and stored until it is needed. Some medical devices and prosthetics can be recycled too. Medical devices like pacemakers, defibrillators, knee and hip replacements, prosthetic limbs, and even breast implants are almost always removed and often discarded before cremation.

By declaring in your funeral pre-planning that you want any device you may have in your body to be removed and donated, you will better the life of someone else. An online search provides several organizations that will accept your used prosthesis, or you can ask a funeral director if they have a recommendation for one.

Service Types

The first thing you need to decide when planning your funeral is what type of funeral service, if any, you want. Six types of funeral services are commonly used to honor the life of someone who has died and to allow your loved ones to say goodbye.

Funeral Service. A funeral service is a formal ceremony that is based on the religious and cultural beliefs of the deceased. The ceremony is for celebrating or remembering the life of a person who has died.

This type of service usually takes place within a few days of the death, at the home of the deceased, in a funeral home, or a church where family and friends come to pay their last respects to the deceased and their immediate family.

At this type of ceremony, the deceased's body must be present and is traditionally not cremated. The remains are moved from their home or the funeral home to the church where the ceremony will take place.

During the ceremony traditionally there are scripture readings, hymns, a short sermon, and a eulogy. The deceased's remains are then moved by procession to the designated location for the burial, or the crematorium for cremation if it wasn't previously done so.

No hard and fast rule states that you must plan your funeral to include specific elements. You are the only one who decides what you want done.

A Memorial Service. A memorial service is a ceremony for celebrating or remembering the life of a person who has already been buried or cremated. The difference between a funeral service and a memorial service is the presence of the deceased's body. Unlike a funeral service, the body of the deceased is not present at a memorial service.

Because the body does not need to be present, a memorial service can be held at any time after the death, from days to a week or even a year. This type of service is often used for celebrations of life, which are usually more informal and non-religious. A memorial service allows family, friends, and acquaintances to come together to celebrate the life of a loved one after their death.

After the initial impact and feelings of grief have subsided, a memorial service can be more of a celebration of your life as opposed to a final goodbye. If you have a special place such as a beach, park, restaurant, or hiking trail, consider holding your memorial service there. After all, this service is about celebrating you and your life.

The memorial service can also be held at a more traditional or religious venue such as a funeral home, church, or temple if you prefer that setting.

A **Committal (Graveside) Service**. Although a funeral service and memorial service might include a committal service (also referred to as a graveside service), some people choose to solely do a committal service.

A committal service is a brief ritual, often involving prayer that takes place at the graveside following a funeral, or in the case of cremation, in the cremation chapel. Flowers are often placed upon the casket by loved ones before the grave is filled with soil.

Viewings and Visitations. In addition to the actual service, often people choose to hold some kind of visitation or viewing. These events are hosted to allow friends and family to visit and express sympathy to your family; or to provide an opportunity to see you one last time and say goodbye.

Private family visitation can allow your family to share their grief in a more personal and intimate setting, outside of the formal ceremony. This helps ease the grieving process and can provide some sense of closure to your family who are grieving. It is generally held at the funeral home but can be held at a family home, church, or some other venue.

A visitation can occur whether the body is present or has been cremated, whereas a viewing is for open-casket funerals. It is generally held at the funeral home but can be held at a family home, church, or some other venue.

A viewing is an event that allows family, friends, and acquaintances to see the person who has died for the last time and say their goodbyes. Viewings usually occur before or during a Visitation.

A **Funeral Reception**. A funeral reception may be held after the formal service. A funeral reception provides guests and family members the opportunity to spend time together and remember the person they have lost in a more casual setting. Many receptions are held at the family's home, though they may be held in church halls, restaurants, or other venues. Dinner is usually served during a funeral reception.

A funeral reception, like a viewing or visitation, can help your loved ones navigate the healing process. They can share memories of you, discuss their loss with others, and find comfort in being around people who are going through the same sorrow.

A **Scattering Service**. A scattering ceremony occurs when you choose to be cremated and have your cremains scattered somewhere, rather than having them kept or buried. Usually, the ashes are scattered into the wind, at a location that was especially important to you.

Scattering ceremonies can be simple or elaborate. You may want your family to scatter your ashes into the ocean or combine them with a tree to plant. The ceremony itself is very similar to a graveside or committal service and it's an appropriate time for your loved ones and friends to say a few words to honor you. You may want your favorite scripture recited, a special prayer said, or a comforting hymn sung.

Keep in mind that, depending on the state you're in, there could be laws surrounding where ashes can be scattered. Be sure to verify with your local county environmental or health service.

Body Disposition

Deciding what to do with your remains after you die is another topic you need to consider. By taking this time to thoroughly consider and pre-plan your funeral you are giving one final gift to your loved ones. You are allowing them to mourn your death and celebrate your life without the stress of planning your funeral.

Your body disposition plan leaves clear instructions about how your remains are handled after you die. If you want to have a huge celebration complete with a piñata, or a jazz marching band parade through your neighborhood, this is the place to record it.

There are several options for disposing of your remains, but the three most common methods used in America are burial, cremation, and donation.

Burial is the traditional method, and it is the most expensive. It usually requires you to purchase a casket, a cemetery plot, and a grave marker. Additional fees associated with a traditional burial include paying someone to open and close the grave. Some states require a vault or grave liner to be purchased as well. This method also includes burial in an above-ground tomb or mausoleum.

Cremation is becoming increasingly popular. Because this method does not require you to purchase a casket or to be embalmed, it is often the least expensive. However, keep in mind that if your body must be held for several days it will need to be refrigerated or embalmed to slow the decaying process which could result in an additional fee.

Cremated remains, also called cremains, are environmentally safe to be scattered, kept at home, or even buried in a cemetery or a columbarium. A columbarium is an above-ground structure that holds cremated remains. Keep in mind that if you wish for your remains to be buried in a cemetery or placed in a columbarium there will be additional costs.

An alternative to burying your ashes in a cemetery would be to have your cremains placed in a biodegradable container and buried in a location that meant something to you.

Donating your body to science is another option for disposing of your remains. You can still have a normal funeral service so friends and loved ones can pay their respects, and then your body will be transported to the medical school or scientific institute where you are donating your remains. Depending on the organization you choose, after some time they may have the body parts that remain cremated and returned to your family.

Not all organizations do this so if this is something you're interested in having done, be sure to ask when you speak to them about the donation and include it in your funeral pre-planning records.

Regardless of the disposition method you choose, your state may have a form that must be completed before carrying out your wishes. Be sure to check online or talk to your funeral home about one. Whichever disposition method you decide, be sure to record your wishes in your funeral pre-planning kit so your family knows what is to be done.

Money Saving Tips

Who doesn't like to save a few dollars, right? There is always a way to cut costs and save a few dollars, even when pre-planning your funeral. Here are a few tips that could save you hundreds of dollars in funeral costs. Just ask your funeral director about them.

If you plan to have a traditional burial, you are going to need a casket. Did you know that you can buy a casket from big box stores like Costco and Sam's Club? The average cost of a basic casket purchased through a funeral home is approximately $2,000. By buying one online or from a big box store you can expect to pay less than $1,000.

If you are set on purchasing a casket from a funeral home, ask to view their inventory of low-cost caskets. The funeral director will likely try to dissuade you from purchasing one in favor of a more expensive one but ask to see them anyway.

Also, you may want to skip the more expensive metal caskets and vaults altogether.

The metal ones that are marketed to keep out air and moisture to slow the decay process tend to explode. Known as exploding casket syndrome, the seal does prevent air from getting in, and out. Over time as your body decomposes it releases gases that, because of the seal, cannot escape the casket. Eventually, those gases build up and lead to the casket exploding.

If you are planning to be cremated another way to save money is to rent a casket from the funeral home. Most funeral homes have caskets that can be rented for the viewing and visitation services then will remove your body for cremation preparation.

If you choose a direct cremation without a viewing or other service where your body is present, the funeral home must offer an inexpensive unfinished wood box or alternative non-metal container that is cremated with your body. Once again, ask your funeral director to see them.

As people become more environmentally conscious, many of them are opting to not be embalmed, saving themselves hundreds of dollars. However, except for a viewing or visitation that will take place several days after your death, embalming is not necessary or legally required.

How to Pay for your Funeral

There are two ways to pay for a funeral: you either pre-plan for it or you don't. Most people die without pre-planning their funeral. Additionally, many people die without life insurance. If this happens, their family is often left in the precarious situation of coming up with the money needed to pay for their funeral before the funeral home will even perform the service.

If they have the money to outright pay for it, they bite the bullet and pay the bill. If they cannot foot the entire bill, they may need to rally multiple friends and family to amass the total amount needed.

Unfortunately, this is not always possible to do. In that situation, your family may be forced to take on debt they may not be able to afford. Many times, this is in the form of a personal loan, or they put the entire funeral bill on a credit card, adding interest to the final cost.

In some cases, your family may be able to be in debt to the funeral home. However, this will not always be an option. Some funeral homes will extend credit to your loved ones to pay for it, but not all will do this. If, after a funeral home has exhausted all other payment options with you, they will perform the services and bill you for the amount due. They may even put you on a monthly payment plan so that eventually the balance is paid off.

Sadly, this is rarely an option anymore because so many funeral homes have had family's default on their payment plan which means the funeral home took a big loss on the services they provided.

In recent years online fundraising websites such as GoFundMe allow people from all over the country to donate money to a cause. If your family is left with no other option, this may be a potential source to raise funds needed to pay for your funeral. Your family may also be forced to operate several traditional fundraisers like car washes or bake sales. These are just some of the many different fundraisers your family can do to raise money very quickly. In general, people are eager to help when they are helping pay for the loss of a loved one.

Additionally, your family could be forced to sell your personal belongings to pay for your funeral. They could have a big yard sale, or estate sale, or rely on websites like Craigslist or Facebook Marketplace to quickly sell personal goods. There are also many apps such as Letgo designed specifically to help users buy and sell personal items.

By taking the steps to pre-plan your funeral you are eliminating potential debt and stress from your loved ones. One of the funeral pre-planning options is to save the money to pay ahead for your funeral. If you religiously put aside a set amount of money each month into a special account specifically earmarked for funeral expenses, you would eventually have enough to pay for all your final expenses.

It's important to note that this method would only be a viable option for those who are very disciplined. If you don't contribute regularly, you'll never reach the total amount needed. Also, you cannot dip into this money at any point for any reason.

The main drawback to considering the savings account option is the fact that it provides no immediate or near-future protection against the cost of your funeral. Since it will take quite a while to save up all the money needed to pay for your final expenses, if something happens to you before you save the full amount, the remaining balance will fall onto someone else to pay.

Many individuals often rely on a life insurance policy to pay their final expenses. However, life insurance should only be used to take care of your family after you die. Instead, why not consider a funeral insurance policy to pay for your final expenses? This type of policy can be purchased directly from a funeral home and can be used anywhere. Once you decide to purchase a funeral insurance policy, you will have two options to pay for it: pay cash for it outright or make payments to pay off the specified balance over a certain period.

After you've made all the required payments, you can rest easy knowing your funeral expense is paid and your family will not be responsible for it.

A bonus of having a funeral insurance policy that pays for your entire funeral is it locks in the price the day the contract is signed. For example, let's say you planned your funeral, and it comes to $12,000. You end up living an additional 20 years and the cost of your funeral has now increased to $22,000. If you have the pre-planned contract and funeral insurance paid, your funeral will only cost what was agreed to in the original contract, and your now $22,000 funeral will be paid in full.

Most funeral insurance policies are transferable from one funeral home to another; however, some are not. If moving is a possibility for you, you will want to make sure to verify that you can take it to a new funeral home before you execute it. If you can't, you can keep your funeral plans with the funeral home you originally pre-planned your funeral with.

Funeral insurance is just a small face value whole life insurance policy. The insurance companies that offer these plans built them to accept some serious health issues so folks who may not be in the greatest of health can still qualify.

If you must use life insurance to pay for your funeral expenses, keep in mind that there are many different types of life insurance, so it is extremely important to consider the right type of life insurance you need. It is important to note that most of the time, term life insurance plans will only insure someone through the age of 80-85. If you think you'll live beyond your early 80's, you'll probably want to consider a permanent life insurance plan.

Some final expense policies require no medical exams, and your acceptance is guaranteed. Above all else, it's critically important that you choose the right type of life policy to ensure your final expenses are paid.

Tips for Veterans

If you are a veteran there are additional things to consider and forms to be completed.

First and foremost, it is important to include a copy of your DD214 with your funeral pre-planning documents. It will be required by your family or the funeral home when applying for your burial benefits from the Department of Veterans Affairs and the National Cemetery Administration. If you have lost your DD214, you can complete a Request Pertaining to Military Records form, the Standard Form 180 to request a copy.

Certain veterans, spouses, and dependents are eligible for specific burial benefits such as a gravesite in one of the 136 national cemeteries that have available space; opening and closing of the grave; perpetual care; a government-issued headstone or marker; a burial flag; and a Presidential Memorial Certificate, **at no cost** to the family. Some Veterans may also be eligible for a burial allowance. Cremated remains are buried in the same manner and with the same honors as casketed remains.

If you wish to be buried in a national cemetery you must complete VA Form 40-10007 before your death. VA Form 40-10007, the Application for Pre-Need Determination of Eligibility for Burial in a VA National Cemetery, is sent to the National Cemetery Scheduling Office where they will verify that you are eligible to be buried in a National Cemetery. Be sure to include a copy of the veteran's DD214 with the application. Once eligibility has been verified, you will receive a letter to include with your funeral pre-planning records.

Table 2.1

Things to Consider When Pre-Planning Your Funeral

•Do you want to be buried or cremated? Do you want a funeral or memorial service?

•What music do you want to play? What flowers do you want?

•What style and color of casket or urn do you want?

•Do you want a eulogy read, and if so, by whom?

•Do you have a clothing preference you want to be buried in?

•Do you want a wake or celebration of life gathering held, if so, where?

•Where do you want to be interned? Do you own a plot? What are your religious preferences?

•Do you want to write your obituary, if not what information do you want to be included in your obituary?

•Where do you want your obituary published? Your hometown?

•Do you want donations to a specific charity instead of flowers?

•Who should be notified of your death?

•Important information to include with pre-planning

•Do you have any pre-paid funeral arrangements? If so, where?

•Have you written a Will? If so, where is it located?

•Who will oversee your funeral arrangements?

•Do you have a Trust? If so, where is it located? Who are your Trustees?

•Do you have any insurance policies? If so, where are they located?

•Do you have a Healthcare Power of Attorney or a Living Will? Is it current? Where is it located?

•Do you have a Durable Power of Attorney? If so, where is it located?

•Include a list of all your financial accounts and insurance policies including company names, account numbers, and contact information.

•Include a list of all your sources of income.

•Have you designated a "Payable on Death" for any of your financial accounts?

•Include a list of passwords and PINs for your executor, representative, or family to access accounts.

•Include a list of your important or valuable assets and real estate property.

•Do you have a safety deposit box? Where is it located and who has a key?

•Where are your tax returns located?

•Include a list of your attorneys, accountants, and insurance agents.

THIS PAGE INTENTIONALLY LEFT BLANK

The Last Will and Testament

A last will and testament is a legal document in which a testator, the person making the Will, dictates what happens to their possessions and assets when they die. Studies show that at any given time between 30-45% of Americans die without a Will. In recent years two very famous and rich musicians made headlines because both died without a Will leaving it up to a judge to decide who will inherit their estate. If you want to have a say in who you want your property, your money, and guardianship of your children, you NEED to have a Will.

You can write your own Will following a bit of research to ensure that you cover all legal requirements in your state. If you have a sizable estate, it may be better for you to use a lawyer to write a detailed in-depth Will to ensure all probate laws are covered. If your estate is simple or you just want to make sure someone inherits something specific it may be easier to write your own Will, which is certainly better than having no Will at all.

Specific Information Required in a Will Include:

1.   A statement that the document is your Last Will and Testament and that it revokes any previously made will or codicil. Also, Include the statement: "I declare that I am of legal age to make this will and that I am sound of mind."

2.   Identify yourself using your full legal name, date of birth, address, and social security number.

3.   Name the executor. An executor is who you name to carry out the directions in your will. Most married people name their spouse as the executor; however, it is not required to do so, and you can name a capable friend instead. Be sure to talk to the person you choose as your executor about their willingness to take on this responsibility before officially naming them as your executor. You will also want to choose an alternate executor if your first choice is unwilling or unable to perform the duties upon your death.

4.   Identify your heirs. If you are married with children, your spouse, life partner, and children are the primary beneficiaries. If you are single and/or have no children, you may want to make provisions for other people. Be sure to identify

them. You can also exclude any heirs you may have here as well.

5. Name a guardian for any minor or dependent children. If your children are of an age where they still require guardianship and have no other natural parent to take care of them, choose a person to take care of your children until they reach the legal age of majority.

6. Assess and divide your property. List your assets, including real estate, bank accounts, retirement accounts, stocks, bonds, and tangible assets then assign your heirs a percentage of your total assets. This is also where you will bequeath (give) something specific to someone if you want.

7. Sign your Will. Some states may only require your signature and two independent witnesses who are not named in your Will, or you can sign your Will in front of a notary

- 83 -

THIS PAGE INTENTIONALLY LEFT BLANK

LAST WILL and TESTAMENT
Sample Templates

LAST WILL AND TESTAMENT

(With Children)

of

___(Your Name)___

I, ___________________________, Social Security Number ____-__-____, being of sound mind and memory, do make and declare this instrument to be my Last Will and Testament, hereby expressly revoking all former Wills and Codicils made by me at any time heretofore, and intended hereby to dispose of all the property of whatever kind and wherever situated which I own, or in which I have any kind of interest at the time of my death.

I.

IDENTITY OF THE FAMILY

At the time of the execution of this will, I am / not married (choose one) (to _________________), hereinafter referred to as my spouse. I have how many (#) living biological children and I have how many (#) biological grandchildren (if you want to name them in your will).

Biological Children:

Biological Grandchildren:

II.

PAYMENT OF EXPENSES

I direct that all the expenses of my last illness, my funeral expenses, and my just personal debts, including any inheritance taxes, transfer taxes, and estate taxes that may be levied by the United States Government or by any state by any reason of my death, shall be paid by my Independent Executor or out of the residue of my estate as soon as conveniently may be done; provided that my Independent Executor, in such Executor's sole discretion, may distribute from time to time any real or personal property in my estate at the time of my death is subject to a lien securing an indebtedness upon it without discharging said indebtedness if, in my Independent Executor's judgment, the condition of my estate so requires. The distributee shall then be considered as having received my estate's equity in the property.

III.

DISPOSITION OF ESTATE

I give, devise, and bequeath all my estate of whatsoever kind and wheresoever situated as follows:

To my son / daughter / husband / friend (choose one, delete the others) ______________________ I leave ______________________________. (Repeat as many times as you want to leave something to someone)

I leave the remainder of my property, both real and personal, tangible and intangible, to (1st Choice). If (1st Choice) should fail to survive me, I leave all my property, both real and personal, tangible and intangible, to (2nd Choice). If (2nd Choice) should fail to survive me, I leave all my property, both real and personal, tangible and intangible, to (3rd Choice).

I may provide additional instructions in a letter to my Independent Executor as to the disposition of some of my personal and household effects. While I hope that the beneficiary named above will abide by my wishes as expressed in the letter, it is merely an expression of my wishes and is not intended to alter the absolute nature of any bequest contained in this, my Last Will and Testament.

Any property of mine that has not been disposed of under the provision of this Will shall go and be distributed to my heirs-in-law determined as of thirty (30) days after the date of my death.

IV.

DEFINITION OF SURVIVAL

Any legatee, devisee, don, person, or beneficiary concerning all or any part of my estate who shall not survive me until thirty days after the date of my death shall be deemed to have predeceased me and shall be treated for the purposes herein as though such person had predeceased me.

V.

APPOINTMENT OF EXECUTOR

I hereby nominate, constitute, and appoint (1st Choice) as Independent Executor of my estate. If (1st Choice) shall predecease me or fail or refuse to qualify, or die, resign, or become unable to serve during the administration of my estate, I hereby nominate, constitute, and appoint (2nd Choice) as Independent Executor, and all powers, duties, and responsibilities granted and imposed upon (1st Choice) shall devolve upon and become exercised by (2nd Choice). If (2nd Choice) shall predecease me or fail or refuse to qualify, or die, resign, or become unable to serve during the administration of my estate, I hereby nominate, constitute, and appoint (3rd Choice) as Independent Executor, and all powers, duties, and responsibilities granted and imposed upon (2nd Choice) shall devolve upon and become exercised by (3rd Choice).

It is my will and desire and I hereby direct that in the administration of my estate, my Independent Executor or any successor shall not be required to furnish any bond of any kind and that no action shall be had in the county court recording of this, my Last Will and Testament, and the return of any inventory, Appraisement, and List of Claims of my estate.

VI.

POWERS OF EXECUTOR

In addition to the powers vested by the law in independent executors, my Independent Executor or any successor named above, shall specifically, without limitation, have the following powers concerning all properties my Independent Executor administers:

I hereby grant unto my Independent Executor and any successor named above, full power and authority over all of my estate and he or she is authorized to sell, manage, and dispose of the same or any part thereof, and in connection with any such sale or transaction, make, execute and deliver proper deeds, assignments and other written instruments and to do all things proper or necessary in the orderly handling and management of my estate.

My Independent Executor or any successor named above shall have full power and authority to comprise, settle, and adjust all debts, claims, and taxes that may be due from owing by my estate.

My Independent Executor or any successor named above shall have full power and authority to deal with any person, firm, or corporation.

In addition to, and not in limitation of, the foregoing, my Independent Executor shall have the powers conferred by law upon personal representatives of estates.

As compensation for his or her services hereunder, my Independent Executor or any successor named above shall be entitled to charge the same fees customarily charged for similar services in other estates at the time services are rendered.

VII.

GUARDIANSHIP

Upon my death, I appoint (my spouse if you have one) _____________________ as sole legal Guardian of _____________________ (name each of your children). If my spouse predeceases me or is unsuitable or ceases to act as Guardian of _______________ (name each of your children), then I appoint (2nd Choice) to act as successor Guardian of _________________ (name each of your children). In the event (2nd Choice) predeceases me or is unsuitable or ceases to act as Guardian of _______________ (name each of your children), then I appoint (3rd Choice) to act as successor Guardian of ___________________ (name each of your children).

VIII.

SPENDTHRIFT PROVISION

No interest of any beneficiary in the corpus or income of my estate shall be subject to assignment, alienation, pledge, attachment, or claims of creditors of such beneficiary and may not otherwise be alienated or encumbered by such beneficiary, except as may be otherwise expressly provided herein.

IX.

IN TERROREM CLAUSE

If any such beneficiary under this Will shall in any manner contest or attack this Will or any of its provisions, any share or interest in my estate given to such contested beneficiary under this Will is hereby revoked and such contesting beneficiary shall receive no part of my estate.

X.

DEFINITIONS AND INTERPRETATIONS

For this, my Last Will and Testament, and the administration of the estate established herein, the following provisions shall apply:

The words "child, children, descendants, issues" and similar terms shall be deemed to include such a person in gestation at the applicable time and later born alive as if that person were living at the applicable time. An adopted person [if adopted before the age of eighteen] and that adopted person's lawful descendants are lawful descendants of anyone who is by blood or adoption an ancestor of that adopting parent.

When a distribution is directed to be made to any person's dependent "per stirpes", that property shall pass equally to that person's children living at the applicable time or all to that person's child if only one is living; providing that if any child that person is not then living but has issues then living, the property which would have passed to that deceased child if he or she were then living shall pass instead to his or her then living, per stirpes, providing further that in determining the class comprised of each issue, no issue of a living personal included in that class shall be included herein.

A provision that property is to pass to a persona's "heirs at law" determined as of a certain time means that the property shall pass to those persons then living who would have been, under the laws of any state in force on the date of this Will, heirs at law of that person's separate personal state, had that person died interstate at the time, in any proportions they would have received the same had been that person's sole heirs in law.

The use of masculine, feminine, or neutral gender shall be interpreted to include the other genders, and the use of either the singular or the plural number shall be interpreted to include the other number unless such an interpretation in a particular case is inconsistent with the general tenor of this instrument. Any reference herein related to my Independent Executor shall include her successors regardless of the gender of the successors.

This Will shall be probated by the laws in the state in which it is filed and should any provisions of the same be held unenforceable or invalid for any reason, the unenforceability or invalidity of the said provision shall not affect the enforceability or validity of any part of this Will.

IN TESTIMONY WHEREOF, I hereunto sign my name to this, my Law Will and Testament, consisting of (how many) (#) typewritten pages, each of which are numbered and initialed by me for identification, all in the presence of two witnesses and a Notary Public.

____

Testator Signature (Sign your name in front of a Notary Public)

Acknowledgement

In the State of ____________

In the County of ______________

Subscribed and sworn to before me by said_____(Your Name)______________, testator, and by said (Witness #1) and (Witness #2), witnesses, this _____ day of _______________, 20___.

____

____

Notary Signature   Notary Seal

My Commission Expires: ______________________

(**Or** sign in front of two witnesses)

____

____

Witness #1   Witness #2

There are two (2) exact copies of this Will.

THIS PAGE INTENTIONALLY LEFT BLANK

LAST WILL AND TESTAMENT

(Without Children)

of

_____(Your Name)_____

I, ______________________________, Social Security Number _____-___-____ , being of sound mind and memory, do make and declare this instrument to be my Last Will and Testament, hereby expressly revoking all former Wills and Codicils made by me at any time heretofore, and intended hereby to dispose of all the property of whatever kind and wherever situated which I own, or in which I have any kind of interest at the time of my death.

I.

IDENTITY OF THE FAMILY

At the time of the execution of this will, I am / not married (choose one) (to ______________________________), hereinafter referred to as my spouse. I have no (0) living biological children.

II.

PAYMENT OF EXPENSES

I direct that all the expenses of my last illness, my funeral expenses, and my just personal debts, including any inheritance taxes, transfer taxes, and estate taxes that may be levied by the United States Government or by any state by any reason of my death, shall be paid by my Independent Executor or out of the residue of my estate as soon as conveniently may be done; provided that my Independent Executor, in such Executor's sole discretion, may distribute from time to time any real or personal property in my estate at the time of my death is subject to a lien securing an indebtedness upon it without discharging said indebtedness if, in my Independent Executor's judgment, the condition of my estate so requires. The distributee shall then be considered as having received my estate's equity on the property.

III.

DISPOSITION OF ESTATE

I give, devise, and bequeath all my estate of whatsoever kind and wheresoever situated as follows:

To my husband/partner/friend/sister (choose one, delete the others) _______________________ I leave _______________________________. (Repeat as many times as you want to leave something to someone)

I leave the remainder of my property, both real and personal, tangible and intangible, to (1st Choice). If (1st Choice) should fail to survive me, I leave all my property, both real and personal, tangible and intangible, to (2nd Choice). If (2nd Choice) should fail to survive me, I leave all my property, both real and personal, tangible and intangible, to (3rd Choice).

I may provide additional instructions in a letter to my Independent Executor as to the disposition of some of my personal and household effects. While I hope that the beneficiary named above will abide by my wishes as expressed in the letter, it is merely an expression of my wishes and is not intended to alter the absolute nature of any bequest contained in this, my Last Will and Testament.

Any property of mine that has not been disposed of under the provision of this Will shall go and be distributed to my heirs-in-law determined as of thirty (30) days after the date of my death.

IV.

DEFINITION OF SURVIVAL

Any legatee, devisee, don, person, or beneficiary concerning all or any part of my estate who shall not survive me until thirty days after the date of my death shall be deemed to have predeceased me and shall be treated for the purposes herein as though such person had predeceased me.

V.

APPOINTMENT OF EXECUTOR

I hereby nominate, constitute, and appoint (1st Choice) as Independent Executor of my estate. If (1st Choice) shall predecease me or fail or refuse to qualify, or die, resign, or become unable to serve during the administration of my estate, I hereby nominate, constitute, and appoint (2nd Choice) as Independent Executor, and all powers, duties, and responsibilities granted and imposed upon (1st Choice) shall devolve upon and become exercised by (2nd Choice). If (2nd Choice) shall predecease me or fail or refuse to qualify, or die, resign, or become unable to serve during the administration of my estate, I hereby nominate, constitute, and appoint (3rd Choice) as Independent Executor, and all powers, duties, and responsibilities granted and imposed upon (2nd Choice) shall devolve upon and become exercised by (3rd Choice).

It is my will and desire and I hereby direct that in the administration of my estate, my Independent Executor or any successor shall not be required to furnish any bond of any kind and that no action shall be had in the county court recording of this, my Last Will and Testament, and the return of any inventory, Appraisement, and List of Claims of my estate.

VI.

POWERS OF EXECUTOR

In addition to the powers vested by the law in independent executors, my Independent Executor or any successor named above, shall specifically, without limitation, have the following powers concerning all properties my Independent Executor administers:

I hereby grant unto my Independent Executor and any successor named above, full power and authority over all of my estate and he or she is authorized to sell, manage, and dispose of the same or any part thereof, and in connection with any such sale or transaction, make, execute and deliver proper deeds, assignments and other written instruments and to do all things proper or necessary in the orderly handling and management of my estate.

My Independent Executor or any successor named above shall have full power and authority to comprise, settle, and adjust all debts, claims, and taxes that may be due from owing by my estate.

My Independent Executor or any successor named above shall have full power and authority to deal with any person, firm, or corporation.

In addition to, and not in limitation of, the foregoing, my Independent Executor shall have the powers conferred by law upon personal representatives of estates.

As compensation for his or her services hereunder, my Independent Executor or any successor named above shall be entitled to charge the same fees customarily charged for similar services in other estates at the time services are rendered.

VII.

SPENDTHRIFT PROVISION

No interest of any beneficiary in the corpus or income of my estate shall be subject to assignment, alienation, pledge, attachment, or claims of creditors of such beneficiary and may not otherwise be alienated or encumbered by such beneficiary, except as may be otherwise expressly provided herein.

VIII.

IN TERROREM CLAUSE

If any such beneficiary under this Will shall in any manner contest or attack this Will or any of its provisions, any share or interest in my estate given to such contested beneficiary under this Will is hereby revoked and such contesting beneficiary shall receive no part of my estate.

IX.

DEFINITIONS AND INTERPRETATIONS

For this, my Last Will and Testament, and the administration of the estate established herein, the following provisions shall apply:

The words "child, children, descendants, issues" and similar terms shall be deemed to include such a person in gestation at the applicable time and later born alive as if that person were living at the applicable time. An adopted person [if adopted before the age of eighteen] and that adopted person's lawful descendants are lawful descendants of anyone who is by blood or adoption an ancestor of that adopting parent.

When a distribution is directed to be made to any person's dependent "per stirpes", that property shall pass equally to that person's children living at the applicable time or all to that person's child if only one is living; providing that if any child that person is not then living but has issues then living, the property which would have passed to that deceased child if he or she were then living shall pass instead to his or her then living, per stirpes, providing further that in determining the class comprised of each issue, no issue of a living personal included in that class shall be included herein.

A provision that property is to pass to a persona's "heirs at law" determined as of a certain time means that the property shall pass to those persons then living who would have been, under the laws of any state in force on the date of this Will, heirs at law of that person's separate personal state, had that person died interstate at the time, in any proportions they would have received the same had been that person's sole heirs in law.

The use of masculine, feminine, or neutral gender shall be interpreted to include the other genders, and the use of either the singular or the plural number shall be interpreted to include the other number unless such an interpretation in a particular case is inconsistent with the general tenor of this instrument. Any reference herein related to my Independent Executor shall include her successors regardless of the gender of the successors.

This Will shall be probated by the laws in the state in which it is filed and should any provisions of the same be held unenforceable or invalid for any reason, the unenforceability or invalidity of the said provision shall not affect the enforceability or validity of any part of this Will.

IN TESTIMONY WHEREOF, I hereunto sign my name to this, my Law Will and Testament, consisting of (how many) (#) typewritten pages, each of which are numbered and initialed by me for identification, all in the presence of two witnesses and a Notary Public.

____

Testator Signature (Sign your name in front of a Notary Public)

Acknowledgement

In the State of ______________

In the County of ____________

Subscribed and sworn to before me by said (your name)______, testator, this ____ day of ______________, 20___.

____

____

Notary Signature   Notary Seal

My Commission Expires: ________________

(**Or** sign in front of two witnesses)

______________   ______________________

Witness #1   Witness #2

There are two (2) exact copies of this Will.

THIS PAGE INTENTIONALLY LEFT BLANK

Information for Veterans

The **Honor Guard** is responsible for rendering Military Funeral Honors for an eligible veteran, free of charge, and is mandated by law. The honor guard consists of not less than two members of the Armed Forces. One member of the detail represents the parent service of the deceased veteran.

The honor detail will perform a ceremony that includes the folding and presenting of the United States Burial Flag to the next of kin and the playing of taps. The veteran's parent service representative will present the flag.

Table 3.1

Who is Eligible for Military Funeral Honors

•Military members on active duty or in the selected reserve.

•Former military members who served on active duty and departed under conditions other than dishonorable.

•Former military members who completed at least one term of enlistment or period of initial obligated service in the reserves and departed under conditions other than dishonorable.

Standard Military Honors

Standard military honors can be provided for enlisted service members by the appropriate branch of service. These honors include a casket team, a firing party, and a bugler. Additionally, some branches of the armed services will use the caisson for service members who have reached the top NCO grade.

The cemetery staff will make the arrangements for military honors when requested by the next of kin or representative. A military chaplain may also be requested.

Full Military Honors

In addition to the standard military honors, certain deceased military veterans may also receive an escort platoon (size varies according to the rank of the deceased), a military band, a caisson, and/or a color guard. All service members who die from wounds received because of enemy action are eligible to receive full military honors.

Verifying Funeral Honors Eligibility

The preferred method for verifying eligibility is your Form DD214. If the DD214 isn't available, any discharge document showing other than dishonorable service can be used. You can request a copy of your DD214 from the National Archives using Form SF180 or by requesting it online by visiting https://www.archives.gov/veterans/military-service-records.

How to Request Military Funeral Honors

If you do not pre-plan your funeral, your funeral director will ask your family about your military service. The funeral director will then contact the appropriate military service to arrange for the funeral honors detail. The funeral director will also assist with receiving your burial flag, the government marker, and any other federal and state burial benefits.

Social Security Lump Sum Death Payment

The Social Security Administration (SSA) will pay a one-time, $255 lump-sum death payment (LSDP) to the surviving spouse or certain minor children of a deceased individual who worked long enough and paid enough into Social Security.

Eligibility for the Social Security Lump Sum Death Benefit:

- Surviving spouse - Eligible if they were living with the deceased, or if they were living apart but receiving certain Social Security benefits based on the deceased's record

- Minor children - Eligible if they are unmarried and (1) age 17 or younger, (2) age 18–19 and in school full time, or (3) any age if they developed a disability at age 21 or younger.

Survivors must apply for the $255 lump sum death payment within two years of the death. You can apply by calling 1-800-772-1213 (TTY 1-800-325-0778), visiting your local Social

Security office, or by completing and mailing form SSA-8 along with the required documents.

An appointment is not required, but if you call ahead and schedule one, it may reduce the time you spend waiting to apply.

You can help by being ready to:

Provide any needed documents and answer the questions listed below.

They may ask you to provide documents to show that you are eligible, such as:

•A birth certificate or other proof of birth.

•Proof of U.S. citizenship or lawful alien status if you were not born in the United States.

•U.S. military discharge paper(s) if you had military service before 1968.

•W-2 forms(s) and/or self-employment tax returns for last year.

•A death certificate for the deceased worker.

Important

The Social Security Administration will accept photocopies of W-2 forms or self-employment tax returns, but they must see the original of most other documents, such as your birth certificate. They will return the documents to you.

Do not delay applying for the lump sum death payment benefit if you do not have all the required documents. They will help you get the documents you need.

What they will ask

- Your name and Social Security number.

- The deceased worker's name, gender, date of birth, and Social Security number.

- The deceased worker's date and place of death.

- Whether the deceased worker ever filed for Social Security benefits, Medicare, or Supplemental Security Income. If so, they will also ask for information on whose Social Security record he or she applied for.

- Whether the deceased worker was unable to work because of illnesses, injuries, or conditions at any time during the 14 months before his or her death If yes, when did he or she become unable to work?

- Whether the deceased worker was ever in active military service. If yes, what were the dates of his or her service?

•Whether the deceased worker worked for the railroad industry for 7 years or more.

•Whether the deceased worker earned Social Security credits under another country's social security system.

•The names, dates of birth (or age), and Social Security numbers, if known, of any of the deceased worker's former spouses, and the dates of the marriages and how and when they ended.

•The names of any of the deceased worker's unmarried children under age 18, age 18-19 and in elementary or secondary school, or disabled before age 22.

•The amount of the deceased worker's earnings in the year of death and the preceding year.

•If the deceased worker had a parent who was dependent on the worker for 1/2 of his or her support at the time of the worker's death.

•Whether the deceased worker and surviving spouse were living together at the time of death.

If you are the surviving spouse, they will also ask

•Whether you have been unable to work because of illnesses, injuries, or conditions at any time within the past 14 months. If yes, they will also ask when you became unable to work.

•Whether you or anyone else ever filed for Social Security benefits, Medicare, or Supplemental Security Income on your behalf. If so, they will also ask for information on whose Social Security record you applied for.

•The names, dates of birth (or age), and social security numbers, if known, of any of your former spouses and the dates of the marriages and how and when they ended.

•If you are not the surviving spouse, they will also ask for the surviving spouse's name and address.

You should have your checkbook or other papers that show your account number at a bank, credit union, or other financial institution so you can sign up to receive your one-time lump sum payment through direct deposit and avoid worries about lost or stolen checks and mail delays.

Contact Information

The Department of Veteran Affairs

www.va.gov

Main Information Line: 1-800-698-2411

Benefits Hotline: 1-800-827-1000

The Social Security Administration

www.ssa.gov

1-800-772-1213

THIS PAGE INTENTIONALLY LEFT BLANK

Funeral Pre-Planning Kit

Funeral Pre-Planning Questionnaire

Personal Information

Date

Prepared __________

First   Name   ______________   Middle

______________ Last ____________

Suffix (e.g., Sr., Jr.) ______   Sex   (M   /   F)

______

Social Security No.______________

Citizenship (country) ____________________

Ancestry ____________________

Ethnic Group/Race______________________

Religion ____________________

Street   Address   _____________________________

Apt./Unit # __________

City   __________________   County

______________ State __________

Zip _________ Country ____________________

Birth Information

Date   of   Birth   ____________ City   of   Birth

____

County ____________

State ______________ Country ____________

Emergency Information

Person to Contact _______________________

Phone _______________________

Physician _______________________

Phone _______________________

Attorney _______________________

Phone _______________________

Persons to Notify

Name_______________________

Phone _______________________

Name_______________________

Phone _______________________

Name_______________________

Phone _______________________

Name_______________________

Phone _______________________

Name_______________________

Phone _______________________

Person Responsible for Funeral Arrangements

Name ____________________________________

Phone _______________________

Address __________________ City _____________

State ______ Zip _____

Attorney

Name ____________________________________

Phone _______________________

Address __________________ City _____________

State ______ Zip _____

Executor of Estate

Name ____________________________________

Phone _______________________

Address ____________________ City ________

State ______ Zip ______

Obituary

Newspaper(s) ____________________________________

Other __________________________

Identify where the following important documents are located:

Will ___________________________

Birth Certificate ___________________________

Marriage License ___________________________

Social Security Card ___________________________

Citizenship papers, if appropriate ___________________________

Military Discharge Papers ___________________________

Life and Other Insurance Policies ___________________________

Deeds and Titles to Property (home, autos, etc.) ___________________________

Bank Account Books ___________________________

Income Tax Returns ___________________________

Certificates of Ownership of Burial Property ___________________________

Bills to be Paid and other Financial Information ___________________________

Safe Deposit Box ___________________________

Financial Institution ___________________________
Phone ___________________________

Address ________________________ City _____________ State
_______ Zip ____

Final disposition:

_______ Whole body burial or entombment

_______ Cremation

_______ Donation to medical science

Organization ________________________________ Phone

____

Address _____________ City ________________ State
___________ Zip _________

Specify disposition of ashes (if applicable):

_______ Burial or entombment at a cemetery

_______ Scattering at cemetery

_______ Deliver to survivors

_______ Other (e.g. burial at sea, scattered in outer space, etc.) _______________________________

Choose a type of Funeral Service Plan:

_______ Traditional

Open or Closed Casket _____________

_______ Memorial

_____ Graveside)

_____ Direct

_____ Do you want only a private family viewing?

Preparation Services and Care (these may be required in your state)

_____ Do you want to have an embalming performed?

_____ Do you want a DNA sample taken?

_____ Do you want an autopsy performed?

The funeral home usually dresses you and applies cosmetics if you choose to have an open casket or a private family viewing. If you do not wish to be dressed and have cosmetics used for viewings, please explain below how you would like to be presented:

____

____

____

____

____

____

Clothing Selections

New

____

____

Existing

____

____

Jewelry

____

____

Clothing Selections to be made by

____

Where to hold your visitation

Funeral Home

____

Church

____

Temple

____

Synagogue

____

Other

____

Transportation

How do you want to be transported between locations?

_____ Funeral Coach or Hearse

_____ Funeral Van

_____ Limousine

No. of People ______

_____ Sedan

No. of People ______

_____ Family will provide transportation

Escort Needed? (Y/N) ______

Instructions ___________________________

Memorial Displays

Description

____

____

____

Special Service Components

Complete this section to provide instructions for special service components such as a 21-gun salute, horse-drawn procession, or the rites of fraternal organizations like Masonic organizations or Veterans of Foreign Wars.

Description

____

____

____

____

Memorial Contributions

Preferred Charity #1: _______________________
Telephone _______________________

Address _______________________ City _______________________
State _______ Zip _______

Preferred Charity #2: _______________________
Telephone _______________________

Address _______________________ City _______________________
State _______ Zip _______

Preferred Charity #3: _______________________
Telephone _______________________

Address _______________________ City _______________________
State _______ Zip _______

Cemetery Information

Complete this section if you want a burial or scattering at a cemetery.

Cemetery: _________________________ Telephone

____

Address _________________ City _________________
State _______ Zip _______

Burial Plot or Property Identification:

____

Section: _________________________

Lot: _________________________

Space: _________________________

Niche (for urn): _________________________

Pallbearers

Name _________________________

Phone _________________________

Name _________________________

Phone _________________________

Name _________________________

Phone _________________________

Name _______________________________________

Phone _______________________________________

Name _______________________________________

Phone _______________________________________

Name _______________________________________

Phone _______________________________________

Music

Title _______________________________________

Artist _______________________________________

Title _______________________________________

Artist _______________________________________

Title _______________________________________

Artist _______________________________________

Title _______________________________________

Artist _______________________________________

Title _______________________________________

Artist _______________________________________

Title _______________________________________

Artist _______________________________________

Performers

Name _________________________________

Phone _________________________________

Name _________________________________

Phone _________________________________

Name _________________________________

Phone _________________________________

Name _________________________________

Phone _________________________________

Name _________________________________

Phone _________________________________

Readings

Title/Author/Location

____

Who Read _________________________________

Title/Author/Location

____

Who Read _________________________________

Title/Author/Location

____

Who Read _________________________________

Title/Author/Location

____

Who Read _______________________________________

Title/Author/Location

____

Who Read _______________________________________

Flowers

Flower Selections _______________________________
Florist _______________

Flower Selections _______________________________
Florist _______________

Flower Selections _______________________________
Florist _______________

Flower Selections _______________________________
Florist _______________

Flower Selections _______________________________
Florist _______________

Casket

Manufacturer _____________________________ Model #

____

Model Name _______________________________ Type of
casket _______________

If Wood Specify Type:

____

If Precious Metal Specify Type:

____

Sealed? (Y/N) _________

If Steel Specify Gauge: ______________

Stainless? (Y/N) ________

Sealed? (Y/N) ________

Cloth covered? (Y/N) ________

Other: _________________________________

Identify lid style:

________ Half Couch (2 pieces)

________ Full Couch (1 piece)

Identify interior features:

Material ______________________________

Color ________________________________

Style (e.g., shirred, tailored, tufted):

____

Special Features:

____

Outer Burial Container:

____

Manufacturer _____________________

Model # __________________

Model Name __________________________

Identify the type of outer burial container:

_____ Grave Box or Grave Line

Specify:(e.g., concrete or wood)

____

Vault _____________

Specify: (e.g., concrete, plastic, wood, composite) _______________

Lawn Crypt Specify: (e.g., concrete or wood)

____

Cremation Urn

Manufacturer ___________________

Model # _____________________

Model Name ___________________

Material Type __________________

Grave Marker

Manufacturer _______________________

Model # _________________________

Model Name __________________________________

Identify the type of grave marker:

______ Grave Marker (flush to the ground)

Specify Material ____________________

______ Monument (upright)

Specify Material ____________________

______ Lawn Crypt

Specify: (e.g., concrete or wood) ____________

Monument

Engraving

____

____

____

Stationery Products

______ Guest Register Book:

Manufacturer: _________________

Style _______________   Quantity _______

_______ Prayer Cards:

Manufacturer: ________________

Style _______________Quantity _______

Verse   to   print   on   Prayer   Cards:

____

____

____

____

_______ Memorial Folders:

Manufacturer: _________________   Style

_______________Quantity _______

Verse   to   print   on   Memorial   Folders:

____

____

____

_______ Prayer Books:

Manufacturer: ________________

Style _______________Quantity _______

_______ Acknowledgment Cards:

Manufacturer: _______________

Style _______________Quantity _______

Additional Personal Information

The following information is used to write your obituary. If you'd prefer, you can write your obituary and include it with your funeral pre-planning documents.

Marital Information

Marital Status (single / married / widowed / divorced / partner)

Name:

____

Suffix (e.g., Sr., Jr.) _______ Social Security No.

____

Living? (Y/N) _______   Birth Date _______

Date of Death _______

Address _______________ City _______________
State _______ Zip _______

Country _________ Telephone _______________
E-Mail _______________________________

Marriage Data

Date of Marriage _________ City _______________
State _______ Country _________

Parents

Father Data

Name_______________________________________

Suffix (e.g., Sr., Jr.) _________ Living? (Y/N) _______

Date of Death _______________

Birth Date ______________

Birthplace _________________________________

Married (Y/N) _______

Spouse Name (if not Mother) ________________

Address ________________ City ________________
State ________ Zip ______

Country __________ Telephone ____________

E-Mail ________________

Mother Data

Name ________________________________

Maiden ________________ Living? (Y/N) _______

Date of Death _______________

Birth Date ______________

Birthplace _________________________________

Married (Y/N) ______

Spouse Name (if not Mother) _________________

Address _______________ City _________________

State _______ Zip _______

Country ___________ Telephone ________________

E-Mail ___________

Child/ren

Child #1

Name _______________________________

Suffix (e.g., Sr., Jr.) ________

Male/Female (M/F) ________

Living? (Y/N) ________

Birth Date ______________

Date of Death ____________

Married? (Y/N) __________

Spouse Name ___________________________

No. of Children ________

Address __________________ City _____________ State _______ Zip _______

Country _______________ Telephone ___________

E-Mail ______________

Child #2

Name _______________________________

Suffix (e.g., Sr., Jr.) _______

Male/Female (M/F) _______

Living? (Y/N) _______

Birth Date _______________

Date of Death _______________

Married? (Y/N) _________

Spouse Name _______________________

No. of Children _______

Address _______________ City _____________

State _______ Zip _______

Country _______________ Telephone _________

E-Mail _______________

Child #3

Name _______________________________

Suffix (e.g., Sr., Jr.) _______

Male/Female (M/F) _______

Living? (Y/N) _______

Birth Date _______________

Date of Death _____________

Married? (Y/N) __________

Spouse Name _________________________________

No. of Children _________

Address ________________ City _____________

State _______ Zip _______

Country _______________ Telephone __________

E-Mail ________________

Child #4

Name ____________________________________

Suffix (e.g., Sr., Jr.) _______

Male/Female (M/F) _________

Living? (Y/N) _________

Birth Date _____________

Date of Death ___________

Married? (Y/N) __________

Spouse Name _________________________________

No. of Children _______

Address ________________ City _____________

State _______ Zip ________

Country ______________ Telephone __________

E-Mail ______________

Siblings

Sibling #1

Name _______________________________

Suffix (e.g., Sr., Jr.) _______

Male/Female (M/F) _______

Living? (Y/N) _______

Birth Date _____________

Date of Death ____________

Married? (Y/N) _________

Spouse Name ________________________

No. of Children ________

Address ________________ City ____________

State _______ Zip _______

Country ______________ Telephone __________

E-Mail ______________

Sibling #2

Name _______________________________

Suffix (e.g., Sr., Jr.) _______

Male/Female (M/F) _______

Living? (Y/N) _______

Birth Date _______________

Date of Death ___________

Married? (Y/N) __________

Spouse Name _______________________________

No. of Children _________

Address _________________ City ____________

State _______ Zip _______

Country _______________ Telephone __________

E-Mail _________________

Sibling #3

Name _______________________________

Suffix (e.g., Sr., Jr.) _______

Male/Female (M/F) _______

Living? (Y/N) _______

Birth Date _______________

Date of Death ___________

Married? (Y/N) _____________

Spouse Name _________________________________

No. of Children __________

Address _________________ City _____________

State ________ Zip ________

Country _______________ Telephone ___________

E-Mail _________________

Sibling #4

Name _____________________________

Suffix (e.g., Sr., Jr.) ________

Male/Female (M/F) ________

Living? (Y/N) ________

Birth Date _______________

Date of Death _____________

Married? (Y/N) _____________

Spouse Name _________________________________

No. of Children __________

Address _________________ City _____________

State ________ Zip ________

Country _______________ Telephone ___________

E-Mail _______________

Grandchildren

No. of Grandchildren _______

No. of Great-Grandchildren _______

No. of Great-Great Grandchildren _______

Special Mentions

____

____

____

____

History of Residences

City / State / Country
____

No. of Years _______
City / State / Country
____

No. of Years _______
City / State / Country
____

No. of Years _______

City / State / Country

____

No. of Years _______

Education

Elementary School

____

City/State____________________

High School ______________________________________

City/State____________________

Year Graduated _______

Undergraduate College

____

City/State____________________

Undergraduate Degree __________________

Year Graduated ______

Graduate College

____

City/State_____________________

Graduate Degree ______________________

Year Graduated ______

Military Record

Branch of Service _______________________

Years Served From ___________ to ___________

Rank _________ Service Number ___________

Wars Served

____

Decorations

____

Branch of Service _______________________

Years Served From ___________to ___________

Rank _________ Service Number ___________

Wars Served

____

Decorations

____

Work History

Retired? (Y/N) _______ Year Retired ___________

Principle occupation _______________________

No. of Years _________

Industries

____

Secondary occupation _______________________

No. of Years _________

Industries

____

Significant Employers

Employer #1 _______________________________
City/State _______________________

Years From ____________ to ____________

Employer #2 _______________________________
City/State _______________________

Years From ____________ to ____________

Employer #3 _______________________________
City/State _______________________

Years From ____________ to ____________

Employer #4 _______________________________
City/State _______________________

Years From ____________ to ____________

Religious Affiliations

Institution #1 ________________________________
City/State ________________

Institution #2 ________________________________
City/State ________________

Institution #3 ________________________________
City/State ________________

Memberships and Public Offices Held

Organization #1 ________________________________
City/State ________________

Position(s) Held

____

Organization #2 ________________________________
City/State ________________

Position(s) Held

____

Organization #3 ________________________________
City/State ________________

Position(s) Held

____

Organization #4 ________________________
City/State ______________
Position(s) Held

____

Notable Accomplishments

Accomplishment #1

____

____

____

Accomplishment #2

____

____

____

Accomplishment #3

____

____

____

Accomplishment #4

NOTES:

THIS PAGE INTENTIONALLY LEFT BLANK

Write Your Own Obituary

Obituaries are a way of remembering the life and achievements of those who have died. Unfortunately, most obituaries are written by our loved ones after we're gone. This can result in a short obituary that's more like a death announcement and not a reflection of the life we lived. If that's all you want when you die, that is fine. But why not write your own obituary? You can share the life and achievements you've had and the power to control how you want to be remembered when you write your own obituary. It will also save time and grief for those you leave behind.

Writing your obituary can be a daunting task. It will bring up a flood of mixed feelings and could take a few drafts before you are satisfied with the outcome. Some people choose to write their obituary while they are in good health, even years before it will be needed.

Others may wait until they are given a life-changing prognosis. No matter when you write your obituary, your loved ones will appreciate that you saved them from added grief and uncertainty by writing it yourself.

There's no right or wrong way to write your own obituary, just begin by reflecting on your life and let the memories flow onto the pages. You will laugh, cry, and even become angry at the memories so have some tissue available. Just remember, this is your chance to share what YOU want in your obituary. Tell YOUR story.

An effectively written obituary goes beyond just listing the facts, and instead seeks to honor your impact on those around you. It will provide solace and a sense of closure to those mourning, and to let the world know what made you special. It is important for your loved ones to celebrate your life and acknowledge their loss with dignity. An obituary is how you can make that happen.

On the next page are two templates to help guide you in writing your own obituary. Be creative and funny. Your obituary doesn't have to be sad or somber. If you were the class clown, let it show.

A Short Obituary Template

Full Name, date of birth, date of death.

[Full Name], [age], of [city, state], died [where/of what] on [date].

[He/She/They] [was/were] born in [city] in [year of birth] to [parents' names]. [First Name] was educated at [school(s)], and then went on to ["work at (workplace name or type of career)," "joining (military branch)," etc.].

[He/She/They] [insert details about your family and/or hobbies and interests].

[First Name] was preceded in death by [name(s)/family members] and is survived by [name(s)/family members].

[1st service name/type] is [date of service #1] at [location of service #1], and the [2nd service name/type] is [date of service #2] at [location of service #2]. Donations to [charity name] would be greatly appreciated.

A Life Story Obituary Template

Full Name, date of birth, date of death.

A few sentences to retell a memorable or colorful event in your life, or what you were best known for.

[Full Name], [age], of [city, state], died [where/of what] on [date].

[He/She/They] [was/were] born in [city] in [year of birth] to [parents' names], who [insert what your loved one remembered most about their parents and/or their childhood]. [Insert a few childhood memories about school, childhood friends, hardships, or anything else that helped make you who you are].

[Name] attended [high school] before ["studying (major) at (university name)," "going to work at (workplace name)," "joining (military branch).

Add a paragraph for any of the prompts below that pertain to you or reflect on an important part of your life.

SPOUSE – [First name] met their beloved, [spouse's name] in [year] [at/while] [location/event]. [Insert story of your meeting or early relationship here.] Excited to start their new lives together, the two were married [date/location].

CHILDREN – [First name] and [partner's first name] were blessed with [number] [of children/child], [Insert children's names], and nothing was more important to them.

GRANDCHILDREN – Though [he/she/they] loved [activity] and [hobby], [First Name]'s most precious thing in life was being grandparent. [He/she/they] treasured their time with their grandkids, never failing to [tradition/habit] or [tradition/habit]. [Insert a favorite story here.]

PETS – [First name] had great love for their furry friends, treating every one like a family member. [Insert story about a beloved pet here.]

FRIENDS – [First name] and [her/his/their] friends were like family to one another. From [activity/memory] to [activity/memory], they were together through it all. [Include another favorite story or two here.]

JOB – [First name] was proud of [her/his/their role] as [job title] at [company name]. Working for the company for [# of years], [insert memory or accomplishment here].

CHURCH/COMMUNITY GROUP – [First name] was an active member of [church/group name], devoting their time and energy to [organization goal].

HOBBIES – Everyone who knew [first name] knew how much [she/he/they] loved [hobby or activity]. [Insert favorite story about hobby here.]

[First name] is lovingly remembered for [her/his/their] [specific quality] and the way that you [always or enjoyed doing something specific]. [Your loved ones] couldn't have asked for a better [parent/grandparent/sibling/etc.] and will be missed every day. [Her/his/their] memory will live on in the hearts of all those who knew [her/him/them].

[First Name] was preceded in death by [name(s)/family members] and is survived by [name(s)/family members].

[1st service name/type] is [date of service #1] at [location of service #1], and the [2nd service name/type] is [date of service #2] at [location of service #2]. Donations to [charity name] would be greatly appreciated.

Practice writing your obituary.

____

____

____

____

____

____

____

____

____

THIS PAGE INTENTIONALLY LEFT BLANK

NOTE:

The following documents are free to download from the Department of the VA website, or through a Google search. Be sure you have the most recent form when you download them to use for your pre-planning records. Please DO NOT use the following documents as they are. You can fill them out for your records, if necessary, but do not submit them to the VA for any burial benefit you are claiming.

INSTRUCTION AND INFORMATION SHEET FOR SF 180, REQUEST PERTAINING TO MILITARY RECORDS

1. General Information. The Standard Form 180, Request Pertaining to Military Records (SF180) is used to request information from military records. Certain identifying information is necessary to determine the location of an individual's record of military service. Please try to answer each item on the SF 180. If you do not have and cannot obtain the information for an item, show "NA," meaning the information is "not available." Include as much of the requested information as you can. To determine where to mail this request see Page 2 of the SF180 for record locations and facility addresses.

Online requests may be submitted to the National Personnel Records Center (NPRC) by a veteran or deceased veteran's next of kin using eVetRecs at http://www.archives.gov/veterans/evetrecs/.

2. Personnel records and Service Treatment Records (STR). Personnel records of military members who were discharged, retired, or died in service **less than 62 years** ago and STR's are in the legal custody of the military service department and are administered in accordance with rules issued by the Department of Defense and the Department of Homeland Security (DHS, Coast Guard). STR's of persons on active duty are generally kept at the local servicing clinic, and usually are available from the Department of Veterans Affairs approximately 40 days after the last day of active duty. (See item 3, Archival Records, if the military member was discharged, retired or died in service over 62 years ago.)

    a. Release of information: Release of information is subject to restrictions imposed by the military services consistent with Department of Defense regulations and the provisions of the Freedom of Information Act (FOIA) and the Privacy Act of 1974. The service member (either past or present) or the member's legal guardian has access to almost any information contained in that member's own record. An authorization signature, of the service member or the member's legal guardian, is needed in Section III of the SF180. Others requesting information from military personnel records and/or STR's must have the release authorization in Section III of the SF 180 signed by the member or legal guardian. If the appropriate signature cannot be obtained, only limited types of information can be provided. If the former member is deceased, surviving next of kin may, under certain circumstances, be entitled to greater access to a deceased veteran's records than a member of the general public. The next of kin may be any of the following: unremarried surviving spouse, father, mother, son, daughter, sister, or brother. Requesters must provide proof of death, such as a copy of a death certificate, letter from funeral home or obituary.

    b. Fees for records: There is no charge for most services provided to service members or next of kin of deceased veterans. A nominal fee is charged for certain types of service. In most instances service fees cannot be determined in advance. If your request involves a service fee, you will be notified as soon as that determination is made.

3. Archival Records. Personnel records of military members who were discharged, retired, or died in service **62 or more years** ago have been transferred to the legal custody of NARA and are referred to as "archival" records.

    a. Release of Information: Archival records are open to the public. The Privacy Act of 1974 does not apply to archival records, therefore, written authorization from the veteran or next of kin is not required. However, in order to protect the privacy of the veteran, his/her family, and third parties named in the records, the personal privacy exemption of the Freedom of Information Act (5 U.S.C. 552 (b) (6)) may still apply and preclude the release of some information.

    b. Fees for Archival Records: Access to archival records is granted by offering copies of the records for a fee (44 U.S.C. 2116 (c)). You will be notified if there is a charge for photocopies of documents contained in the record you are requesting.

4. Where reply may be sent. The reply may be sent to the service member or any other address designated by the service member or other authorized requester.

5. Definitions and abbreviations. DISCHARGED -- the individual has no current military status; SERVICE TREATMENT RECORD (STR) -- The chronology of medical, mental health and dental care received by service members during the course of their military career (does not include records of treatment while hospitalized); TDRL -- Temporary Disability Retired List.

6. Service completed before World War I. National Archives Trust Fund (NATF) forms must be used to request these records. Obtain the forms by e-mail from *inquire@nara.gov* or write to the Code 6 address on page 2 of the SF 180.

PRIVACY ACT OF 1974 COMPLIANCE INFORMATION

The following information is provided in accordance with 5 U.S.C. 552a(e)(3) and applies to this form. Authority for collection of the information is 44 U.S.C. 2907, 3101, and 3103, and Public Law 104-134 (April 26, 1996), as amended in title 31, section 7701. Disclosure of the information is voluntary. If the requested information is not provided, it may delay servicing your inquiry because the facility servicing the service member's record may not have all of the information needed to locate it. The purpose of the information on this form is to assist the facility servicing the records (see the address list) in locating the correct military service record(s) or information to answer your inquiry. This form is then retained as a record of disclosure. The form may also be disclosed to Department of Defense components, the Department of Veterans Affairs, the Department of Homeland Security (DHS, U.S. Coast Guard), or the National Archives and Records Administration when the original custodian of the military health and personnel records transfers all or part of those records to that agency. If the service member was a member of the National Guard, the form may also be disclosed to the Adjutant General of the appropriate state, District of Columbia, or Puerto Rico, where he or she served.

PAPERWORK REDUCTION ACT PUBLIC BURDEN STATEMENT

Public burden reporting for this collection of information is estimated to be five minutes per request, including time for reviewing instructions and completing and reviewing the collection of information. Send comments regarding the burden estimate or any other aspect of the collection of information, including suggestions for reducing this burden, to National Archives and Records Administration (NHP), 8601 Adelphi Road, College Park, MD 20740-6001. DO NOT SEND COMPLETED FORMS TO THIS ADDRESS. SEND COMPLETED FORMS AS INDICATED IN THE ADDRESS LIST ON PAGE 2 OF THE SF 180.

<table>
<tr><td>Standard Form 180 (Rev. 09/08) (Page 1)
Prescribed by NARA (36 CFR 1228.168(b))</td><td>Authorized for local reproduction
Previous edition unusable</td><td>OMB No. 3095-0029 Expires 10/31/2011</td></tr>
</table>

REQUEST PERTAINING TO MILITARY RECORDS

* Requests from veterans or deceased veteran's next-of-kin may be submitted online by using eVetRecs at http://www.archives.gov/veterans/evetrecs/ *

(To ensure the best possible service, please thoroughly review the accompanying instructions before filling out this form. Please print clearly or type.)

SECTION I - INFORMATION NEEDED TO LOCATE RECORDS (Furnish as much as possible.)

1. NAME USED DURING SERVICE (last, first, and middle)	2. SOCIAL SECURITY NO.	3. DATE OF BIRTH	4. PLACE OF BIRTH

5. SERVICE, PAST AND PRESENT   (For an effective records search, it is important that all service be shown below.)

	BRANCH OF SERVICE	DATE ENTERED	DATE RELEASED	OFFICER	ENLISTED	SERVICE NUMBER (If unknown, write "unknown")
a. ACTIVE COMPONENT						
b. RESERVE COMPONENT						
c. NATIONAL GUARD						

6. IS THIS PERSON DECEASED? If "YES" enter the date of death.   ☐ NO   ☐ YES ______

7. IS (WAS) THIS PERSON RETIRED FROM MILITARY SERVICE?   ☐ NO   ☐ YES

SECTION II – INFORMATION AND/OR DOCUMENTS REQUESTED

1. CHECK THE ITEM(S) YOU WOULD LIKE TO REQUEST A COPY OF:

☐ **DD Form 214 or equivalent.** This form contains information normally needed to verify military service. A copy may be sent to the veteran, the deceased veteran's next of kin, or other persons or organizations if authorized in Section III, below. NOTE: If more than one period of service was performed, even in the same branch, there may be more than one DD214. **Check the appropriate box below to specify a deleted or undeleted copy.** When was the DD Form(s) 214 issued? YEAR(S): ______

☐ **UNDELETED:** Ordinarily required to determine eligibility for benefits. Sensitive items, such as, the character of separation, authority for separation, reason for separation, reenlistment eligibility code, separation (SPD/SPN) code, and dates of time lost are usually shown.

☐ **DELETED:** The following items are deleted: authority for separation, reason for separation, reenlistment eligibility code, separation (SPD/SPN) code, and for separations after June 30, 1979, character of separation and dates of time lost.

☐ **All Documents in Official Military Personnel File (OMPF)**

☐ **Medical Records** (Includes Service Treatment Records (outpatient), inpatient and dental records.) If hospitalized, provide facility name and date for each admission: ______

☐ **Other** (Specify): ______

2. PURPOSE: (An explanation of the purpose of the request is **strictly voluntary**; however, such information may help to provide the best possible response and may result in a faster reply. Information provided will in no way be used to make a decision to deny the request.) Check appropriate box:

☐ Benefits   ☐ Employment   ☐ VA Loan Programs   ☐ Medical   ☐ Medals/Awards   ☐ Genealogy   ☐ Correction   ☐ Personal
☐ Other, explain: ______

SECTION III - RETURN ADDRESS AND SIGNATURE

1. REQUESTER IS: *(Signature Required in # 3 below of veteran, next of kin, legal guardian, authorized government agent or "other" authorized representative. If "other" authorized representative, provide copy of authorization letter.)*

☐ Military service member or veteran identified in Section I, above

☐ Next of kin of deceased veteran (Must provide proof of death).
    Show relationship: ______

☐ Legal guardian (Must submit copy of court appointment.)

☐ Other (specify) ______

(See item 2a on accompanying instructions.)

2. SEND INFORMATION/DOCUMENTS TO:
(Please print or type. See item 4 on accompanying instructions.)

3. AUTHORIZATION SIGNATURE REQUIRED *(See items 2a or 3a on accompanying instructions.)* I declare (or certify, verify, or state) under penalty of perjury under the laws of the United States of America that the information in this Section III is true and correct.

Name ______

Street ______ Apt. ______

City ______ State ______ Zip Code ______

Signature Required - Do not print

Date of this request ______ Daytime phone ( ) ______

Email address ______

*This form is available at *http://www.archives.gov/research/order/standard-form-180.pdf* on the National Archives and Records Administration (NARA) web site.*

<table>
<tr><td>Standard Form 180 (Rev. 09/08) (Page 2)
Prescribed by NARA (36 CFR 1228.168(b))</td><td>Authorized for local reproduction
Previous edition unusable</td><td>OMB No. 3095-0029 Expires 10/31/2011</td></tr>
</table>

LOCATION OF MILITARY RECORDS

The various categories of military service records are described in the chart below. For each category there is a code number which indicates the address at the bottom of the page to which this request should be sent. Please refer to the Instruction and Information Sheet accompanying this form as needed.

BRANCH	CURRENT STATUS OF SERVICE MEMBER	ADDRESS CODE	
		Personnel Record	Service Treatment Record
AIR FORCE	Discharged, deceased, or retired before 5/1/1994	14	14
	Discharged, deceased, or retired 5/1/1994 – 9/30/2004	14	11
	Discharged, deceased, or retired on or after 10/1/2004	1	11
	Active (including National Guard on active duty in the Air Force), TDRL, or general officers retired with pay	1	
	Reserve, retired reserve in nonpay status, current National Guard officers not on active duty in the Air Force, or National Guard released from active duty in the Air Force	2	
	Current National Guard enlisted not on active duty in the Air Force	13	
COAST GUARD	Discharge , deceased, or retired before 1/1/1898	6	
	Discharged, deceased, or retired 1/1/1898 – 3/31/1998	14	14
	Discharged, deceased, or retired on or after 4/1/1998	14	11
	Active, reserve, or TDRL	3	
MARINE CORPS	Discharged, deceased, or retired before 1/1/1905	6	
	Discharged, deceased, or retired 1/1/1905 – 4/30/1994	14	14
	Discharged, deceased, or retired 5/1/1994 – 12/31/1998	14	11
	Discharged, deceased, or retired on or after 1/1/1999	4	11
	Individual Ready Reserve	5	
	Active, Selected Marine Corps Reserve, TDRL	4	
ARMY	Discharged, deceased, or retired before 11/1/1912 (enlisted) or before 7/1/1917 (officer)	6	
	Discharged, deceased, or retired 11/1/1912 – 10/15/1992 (enlisted) or 7/1/1917 – 10/15/1992 (officer)	14	14
	Discharged, deceased, or retired after 10/16/1992	14	11
	Reserve; or active duty records of current National Guard members who performed service in the U.S. Army before 7/1/1972	7	
	Active enlisted (including National Guard on active duty in the U.S. Army) or TDRL enlisted	9	
	Active officers (including National Guard on active duty in the U.S. Army) or TDRL officers	8	
	Current National Guard enlisted and officer not on active duty in Army (including records of Army active duty performed after 6/30/1972)	13	
NAVY	Discharged, deceased, or retired before 1/1/1886 (enlisted) or before 1/1/1903 (officer)	6	
	Discharged, deceased, or retired 1/1/1886 – 1/30/1994 (enlisted) or 1/1/1903 – 1/30/1994 (officer)	14	14
	Discharged, deceased, or retired 1/31/1994 – 12/31/1994	14	11
	Discharged, deceased, or retired on or after 1/1/1995	10	11
	Active, reserve, or TDRL	10	
PHS	Public Health Service - Commissioned Corps officers only	12	

ADDRESS LIST OF CUSTODIANS (BY CODE NUMBERS SHOWN ABOVE) – Where to write/send this form

1	Air Force Personnel Center HQ AFPC/DPSSRP 550 C Street West, Suite 19 Randolph AFB, TX 78150-4721	6	National Archives & Records Administration Old Military and Civil Records (NWCTB-Military) Textual Services Division 700 Pennsylvania Ave., N.W. Washington, DC 20408-0001	11	Department of Veterans Affairs Records Management Center P.O. Box 5020 St. Louis, MO 63115-5020
2	Air Reserve Personnel Center /DSMR HQ ARPC/DPSSA/B 6760 E. Irvington Place, Suite 4600 Denver, CO 80280-4600	7	U.S. Army Human Resources Command ATTN: AHRC-PAV-V 1 Reserve Way St. Louis, MO 63132-5200	12	Division of Commissioned Corps Officer Support ATTN: Records Officer 1101 Wooton Parkway, Plaza Level, Suite 100 Rockville, MD 20852
3	Commander, CGPC-adm-3 USCG Personnel Command 4200 Wilson Blvd., Suite 1100 Arlington, VA 22203-1804	8	U.S. Army Human Resources Command ATTN: AHRC-MSR 200 Stovall Street Alexandria, VA 22332-0444	13	The Adjutant General (of the appropriate state, DC, or Puerto Rico)
4	Headquarters U.S. Marine Corps Personnel Management Support Branch (MMSB-10) 2008 Elliot Road Quantico, VA 22134-5030	9	Commander USAEREC ATTN: PCRE-F 8899 E. 56th St. Indianapolis, IN 46249-5301	14	National Personnel Records Center (Military Personnel Records) 9700 Page Ave. St. Louis, MO 63132-5100 *http://www.archives.gov/veterans/evetrecs/*
5	Marine Corps Mobilization Command 15303 Andrews Road Kansas City, MO 64147-1207	10	Navy Personnel Command (PERS-312E) 5720 Integrity Drive Millington, TN 38055-3120		

 **Department of
Veterans Affairs**

INSTRUCTIONS FOR COMPLETING APPLICATION FOR BURIAL BENEFITS
(UNDER 38 U.S.C., CHAPTER 23)

IMPORTANT - READ THESE INSTRUCTIONS CAREFULLY

PRIVACY ACT INFORMATION: The responses you submit are considered confidential (38 U.S.C. 5701). They may be disclosed outside the Department of Veterans Affairs (VA) only if the disclosure is authorized under the Privacy Act, including the routine uses identified in the VA system of records, 58VA21/22/28, Compensation, Pension, Education and Vocational Rehabilitation and Employment Records - VA, published in the Federal Register. The requested information is considered relevant and necessary to determine maximum benefits under the law and is required to obtain benefits. Information submitted is subject to verification through computer matching programs with other agencies.

RESPONDENT BURDEN: We need this information to determine your eligibility to burial benefits. Title 38, United States Code, allows us to ask for this information. We estimate that you will need an average of 15 minutes to review the instructions, find the information, and complete this form. VA cannot conduct or sponsor a collection of information unless a valid OMB control number is displayed. Valid OMB control numbers can be located on the OMB Internet Page at www.reginfo.gov/public/do/PRAMain. If desired, you can call 1-800-827-1000 to get information on where to send comments or suggestions about this form.

1. GENERAL

   a. ELIGIBILITY - NON-SERVICE-CONNECTED

      (1) NON-SERVICE-CONNECTED BURIAL ALLOWANCE - A one-time payment for a veteran who was receiving VA pension or disability compensation; would have been receiving disability compensation but for the receipt of military retired pay, or had an eligible pending claim at the time of death.

      (2) SERVICE-CONNECTED BURIAL ALLOWANCE - A one-time payment for a veteran who was rated totally disabled for a service-connected disability or disabilities; excluding individual unemployability, or who died of a service-connected disability.

      (3) VA MEDICAL CENTER DEATH BURIAL ALLOWANCE - A one-time payment for a veteran whose death was not service-connected and who died while hospitalized by VA.

   b. BURIAL ALLOWANCE - A one-time benefit payment payable toward the expenses of the funeral and burial of the veteran's remains. Burial includes all legal methods of disposing of the veteran's remains including, but not limited to, cremation, burial at sea, and medical school donation.

   c. PLOT OR INTERMENT ALLOWANCE - A one-time benefit payment payable toward:

      (1) Expenses incurred for the plot or interment if burial was not in a national cemetery or other cemetery under the jurisdiction of the United States; OR

      (2) Expenses payable to a State (or political subdivision of a State) if the veteran died from non-service-connected causes and was buried in a State-owned cemetery or section used solely for the remains of persons eligible for burial in a national cemetery.

"Plot" means the final disposition site of the remains, whether it is a grave, mausoleum vault, columbarium niche, or <u>similar place</u>. "<u>Interment</u>" means the burial of casketed remains in the ground or the <u>placement</u> of cremated remains into a columbarium niche.

   d. TRANSPORTATION EXPENSES - The cost of transporting the body to the place of burial may be paid in addition to the burial allowance when:

      (1) The veteran died of a service-connected disability or had a compensable service-connected disability and burial is in a national cemetery; OR

      (2) The veteran died while in a hospital, domiciliary or nursing home to which he/she had been properly admitted under authority of VA; OR

      (3) The veteran died en route while traveling under prior authorization of VA for the purpose of examination, treatment; OR

      (4) The veteran's remains are unclaimed and burial is in a national cemetery.

2. **WHO SHOULD FILE A CLAIM** - VA may grant a claim that any eligible person files. Upon death of the veteran, VA will pay the first living person to file a claim of those listed below:

   (1) The veteran's surviving spouse; OR
   (2) The survivor of a legal union* between the deceased veteran and the survivor; OR
   (3) The veteran's children, regardless of age; OR
   (4) The veteran's parents or the surviving parent; OR
   (5) The executor or administrator of the deceased veteran's estate, or person acting for the deceased veteran's estate.

   *For purposes of this application, <u>legal union</u> means a formal relationship between the veteran and the survivor that existed on the date of the veteran's death, was recognized under the law of the State in which the couple formalized the relationship, and was evidenced by the State's issuance of documentation memorializing the relationship.

   If the veterans remains are unclaimed, VA will pay the person or entity that provided burial services for the remains of an unclaimed veteran.

3. **TIME LIMIT FOR FILING A CLAIM** - A claim for non-service-connected burial allowance must be filed with VA within 2 years after the date of the veteran's permanent burial or cremation. If a veteran's discharge was corrected after death to "Under Conditions Other Than Dishonorable," the claim must be filed within 2 years after the date of correction. There is no time limit for the service-connected burial allowance, plot or interment allowance, VA hospitalization death burial allowance, or reimbursement of transportation expenses.

4. **COMPLETING CLAIM BY A FIRM OR STATE AGENCY** - The claim must be executed in the full name of the firm or State agency, and show the official position or connection of the individual who signs on its behalf.

5. **PROOF OF DEATH TO ACCOMPANY CLAIM** - Death in a government institution does not need to be proven. In other cases, the claimant must forward a copy of the public record of death. If proof has previously been furnished VA, it need not be submitted again.

6. **STATEMENT OF ACCOUNT MUST ACCOMPANY TRANSPORTATION CLAIMS** - If transported by common carrier, a receipt must accompany the claim. All receipts for transportation charges should show the name of the veteran, the name of the person who paid, and the amount of the charges. The itemized statement of account should show the charges made for transportation. Failure to itemize charges may result in delay or payment of a lesser amount.

7. **SERVICE RECORD** - The original or certified copy of the veteran's service separation document (DD214 or equivalent) which contains information as to the length, time, and character of service will permit prompt processing.

8. **TOLL-FREE TELEPHONE ASSISTANCE** - You can call us toll-free within the U.S. by dialing 1-800-827-1000. If you are located in the local dialing area of a VA regional office, you can also call us by checking your local telephone directory. For the hearing impaired, our TDD number is 711.

9. **WHERE DO I MAIL MY COMPLETED APPLICATION?** - You should mail your application to the VA regional office located in your state. You can obtain the mailing address for VA regional offices by accessing the VA Internet web site at www.va.gov/directory. The address is also located in the government pages of your telephone book under "United States Government, Veterans."

OMB Approved No. 2900-0003
Respondent Burden: 15 Minutes
Expiration Date: 04/30/2020

Department of Veterans Affairs

APPLICATION FOR BURIAL BENEFITS
(Under 38 U.S.C. Chapter 23)

IMPORTANT - Read instructions carefully before completing form. **YOUR COMPLIANCE WITH ALL INSTRUCTIONS WILL AVOID DELAY. Type or print all information.**

NOTE: You can *either* complete the form online or by hand. Please print information using blue or black ink, neatly, and legibly to help process the form.

(DO NOT WRITE IN THIS SPACE)
(VA DATE STAMP)

PART I - PERSONAL INFORMATION

1. FIRST, MIDDLE, LAST NAME OF DECEASED VETERAN'S NAME

2. VETERAN'S SOCIAL SECURITY NUMBER

3. VA FILE NUMBER

C/CSS -

CLAIMANT'S PERSONAL INFORMATION

4. CLAIMANT'S NAME *(First, middle initial, last)*

5. CURRENT MAILING ADDRESS *(Number and street or rural route, P.O. Box, City, State, ZIP Code and Country)*

No. & Street

Apt./Unit Number

City

State/Province

Country

ZIP Code/Postal Code

6. PREFERRED TELEPHONE NUMBER *(Include Area Code)*

7. PREFERRED E-MAIL ADDRESS

8. RELATIONSHIP OF CLAIMANT TO DECEASED VETERAN *(Check one)*

- [ ] SPOUSE
- [ ] CHILD
- [ ] PARENT
- [ ] EXECUTOR/ADMINISTRATOR OF ESTATE OR PERSON ACTING FOR THE ESTATE
- [ ] OTHER *(Specify)*

PART II - INFORMATION REGARDING VETERAN

9A. DATE OF BIRTH

9B. PLACE OF BIRTH

10A. DATE OF DEATH

10B. PLACE OF DEATH

10C. DATE OF BURIAL

SERVICE INFORMATION *(The following information should be furnished for the periods of the VETERAN'S ACTIVE SERVICE)*

11A. ENTERED SERVICE		11B. SERVICE NUMBER	11C. SEPARATED FROM SERVICE		11D. GRADE, RANK OR RATING, ORGANIZATION AND BRANCH OF SERVICE
DATE	PLACE		DATE	PLACE	

12. IF VETERAN SERVED UNDER NAME OTHER THAN THAT SHOWN IN ITEM 1, GIVE FULL NAME AND SERVICE RENDERED UNDER THAT NAME

VA FORM
APR 2017 **21P-530**

SUPERSEDES VA FORM 21P-530, JUN 2015, WHICH WILL NOT BE USED

Page 3

VETERAN'S SSN ☐☐☐ — ☐☐ — ☐☐☐☐

PART III - CLAIM FOR BURIAL ALLOWANCE

13A. TYPE OF BURIAL ALLOWANCE REQUESTED *(Check one)*

☐ NON-SERVICE-CONNECTED DEATH

☐ SERVICE-CONNECTED DEATH

☐ VA MEDICAL CENTER DEATH *(See instructions for definition.)*

(If VA Medical Center Death is checked, provide actual burial cost.)

$

13B. WHERE DID THE VETERAN'S DEATH OCCUR? *(Check one)*

☐ VA MEDICAL CENTER   ☐ NURSING HOME UNDER VA CONTRACT

☐ STATE VETERANS HOME   ☐ OTHER *(Specify)*

14. IF YOU ARE THE DECEASED VETERAN'S SPOUSE, DID YOU PREVIOUSLY RECEIVE A VA BURIAL ALLOWANCE?

☐ YES ☐ NO

15A. DID YOU INCUR EXPENSES FOR THE VETERAN'S BURIAL?

☐ YES ☐ NO

15B. ARE YOU SEEKING BURIAL BENEFITS FOR THE UNCLAIMED REMAINS OF A VETERAN?

☐ YES ☐ NO

PART IV - CLAIM FOR PLOT OR INTERMENT ALLOWANCE

16. PLACE OF BURIAL OR LOCATION OF DECEASED VETERAN'S REMAINS
(Specify)

17A. DID YOU INCUR EXPENSES FOR THE VETERAN'S PLOT OR INTERMENT?

☐ YES ☐ NO

17B. WAS VETERAN BURIED IN A NATIONAL CEMETERY, OR ONE OWNED BY THE FEDERAL GOVERNMENT?

☐ YES ☐ NO

17C. WAS THE VETERAN BURIED IN A STATE VETERANS CEMETERY?

☐ YES ☐ NO

18A. DID A FEDERAL/STATE GOVERNMENT OR THE VETERAN'S EMPLOYER CONTRIBUTE TO THE BURIAL?

☐ YES ☐ NO *(If "Yes," complete Item 18B)*

18B. AMOUNT OF GOVERNMENT OR EMPLOYER CONTRIBUTION

$

PART V - CLAIM FOR TRANSPORTATION REIMBURSEMENT

19. EXPENSES INCURED FOR THE TRANSPORTATION OF THE VETERAN'S REMAINS FROM THE PLACE OF DEATH TO THE FINAL RESTING PLACE
(Attach itemized receipts)

$

PART VI - CERTIFICATION AND SIGNATURE

I CERTIFY THAT the foregoing statements made in connection with this application on account of the named veteran are true and correct to the best of my knowledge and belief.

20A. SIGNATURE OF CLAIMANT *(Sign in ink)* *(If signed using an "X", complete Items 22A thru 23B)* *(If signing for firm, corporation, or State agency, complete Items 20B thru 21)*

20B. OFFICIAL POSITION OF PERSON SIGNING ON BEHALF OF FIRM, CORPORATION OR STATE AGENCY *(Please sign in ink.)*

21. FULL NAME AND ADDRESS OF THE FIRM, CORPORATION, OR STATE AGENCY FILING AS CLAIMANT

WITNESS TO SIGNATURE IF MADE BY "X"

NOTE - If claimant signed above using an "X", signature must be witnessed by two persons to whom the person making the statement is personally known, and the signatures and addresses of such witnesses must be shown below.

22A. SIGNATURE OF WITNESS *(Sign in ink.)*

22B. ADDRESS OF WITNESS

23A. SIGNATURE OF WITNESS *(Sign in ink.)*

23B. ADDRESS OF WITNESS

PENALTY - The law provides severe penalties which include fine or imprisonment, or both, for the willful submission of any statement or evidence of a material fact knowing it to be false.

DEPARTMENT OF VETERANS AFFAIRS HEADSTONES AND MARKERS

The Department of Veterans Affairs will furnish, upon request, a Government headstone or marker at the expense of the United States for the unmarked graves of certain individuals eligible for burial in a national cemetery, but not buried there. These individuals may include any veterans with an other than dishonorable discharge who dies after service or any servicemember who dies on active duty. Certain other individuals may also be eligible for the headstone or marker. Headstones or markers for all individuals in a national or post cemetery are furnished automatically without request from the family.

For additional information on burial benefits go to the web site, www.cem.va.gov/bbene_burial.asp. To obtain VA Form 40-1330, Application for Standard Government Headstone or Marker go to www.va.gov/vaforms or contact your local VA regional office. The address of that office can be found at to www.va.gov/directory.

OMB NUMBER: 2900-0784
EXPIRATION DATE: November 30, 2018
RESPONDENT BURDEN: 20 minutes

Department of Veterans Affairs

APPLICATION FOR PRE-NEED DETERMINATION OF ELIGIBILITY FOR BURIAL IN A VA NATIONAL CEMETERY

NOTE: Please read information on reverse before completing this form. If additional space is required, attach a separate sheet of paper.

Submit Application and Supporting Documentation to VA by:
Mail: to National Cemetery Scheduling Office, P.O. Box 510543, St. Louis, MO 63151; or
Fax: to the National Cemetery Scheduling Office at (855) 840-8299

IMPORTANT: Pre-Need means before death. Only complete this form if you are applying for a Pre-Need determination of eligibility for burial in a VA national cemetery. Time of Need means time of death. DO NOT complete this form if the individual is already deceased; instead, contact a local funeral home or the National Cemetery Scheduling Office at 1-800-535-1117 to expedite processing.

***REQUIRED ITEMS: YOU MUST COMPLETE THOSE ITEMS IDENTIFIED WITH AN ASTERISK (*)**

SECTION I - VETERAN/SERVICEMEMBER
(Claims for eligibility for burial are based upon the Veterans/Servicemember's military service)

***1. VETERAN/SERVICEMEMBER NAME** *(Include Suffix) (Last, First, Middle Name or Initial)*

***2. NAME USED DURING MILITARY SERVICE** *(Include Suffix) (If different than Item 1) (Last, First, Middle Name)*

3. MAILING ADDRESS *(Street, City, State, and Zip Code, P.O. Box, Rural Route, etc.)*

***4. SOCIAL SECURITY NUMBER**

5. MILITARY SERVICE NUMBER *(If different from SSN)*

6. VA CLAIM NUMBER *(If known)*

***7. GENDER** ☐ MALE ☐ FEMALE

8. DATE OF BIRTH *(MM/DD/YYYY)*

9. PLACE OF BIRTH *(City, State or Territory)*

***10. IS VETERAN/SERVICEMEMBER DECEASED?** ☐ YES ☐ NO ☐ DON'T KNOW

11. DATE OF DEATH *(If applicable) (MM/DD/YYYY)*

***12. MARITAL STATUS** ☐ SINGLE ☐ SEPARATED ☐ MARRIED ☐ DIVORCED ☐ WIDOWED

***13. MILITARY STATUS USED TO APPLY FOR ELIGIBILITY DETERMINATION** *(Check all that apply)*
☐ A. VETERAN ☐ B. RETIRED ACTIVE DUTY ☐ C. DIED ON ACTIVE DUTY ☐ D. RETIRED RESERVE
☐ E. RETIRED NATIONAL GUARD ☐ F. DEATH RELATED TO INACTIVE DUTY TRAINING ☐ G. OTHER *(See instructions)*

MILITARY SERVICE DATA

*14. BRANCH OF SERVICE	15. DATE OF ENTRY	16. DATE OF DISCHARGE	17. DISCHARGE - CHARACTER OF SERVICE *(See instructions)*	18. HIGHEST RANK ATTAINED *(No pay grades)*	19. STATE *(Abbrev.)* *(National Guard Service Only)*

20. IS THERE ANYONE CURRENTLY BURIED IN A VA NATIONAL CEMETERY UNDER THIS VETERAN'S/SERVICEMEMBER'S ELIGIBILITY?
☐ YES *(Complete Item 21)* ☐ NO *(Skip Item 21)* ☐ DON'T KNOW *(Skip Item 21)*

21. NAME OF DECEDENT(S) AND VA NATIONAL CEMETERY WHERE BURIED

22. SUPPORTING DOCUMENTS ATTACHED ☐ YES ☐ NO *(See instructions for information on recommended documentation.)*

SECTION II - CLAIMANT INFORMATION
(Information about the individual for whom determination for eligibility for burial in a VA National Cemetery is requested)

23. CLAIMANT** *(See instructions) (Each Claimant requires a separate VA Form 40-10007)*

(Name) Last   First   Middle

WHO IS *(check one)*:
☐ A. THE VETERAN/SERVICEMEMBER NAMED IN ITEM 1
☐ B. THE SPOUSE/SURVIVING SPOUSE OF THE VETERAN/SERVICEMEMBER IN ITEM 1
☐ C. AN UNMARRIED ADULT CHILD OF THE VETERAN/SERVICEMEMBER IN ITEM 1
☐ D. OTHER *(Please specify)*

***24. CLAIMANT'S MAILING ADDRESS** *(Street, City, State, and Zip Code, P.O. Box, Rural Route, etc.) (If different from item 3)*

25. CLAIMANT'S TELEPHONE NUMBER *(Include Area Code)*

***26. CLAIMANT'S SOCIAL SECURITY NUMBER** *(If different from item 4)*

***27. CLAIMANT'S DATE OF BIRTH** *(MM/DD/YYYY) (If different from item 8)*

***28. CLAIMANT'S MAIDEN NAME** *(If applicable)*

29. DESIRED VA NATIONAL CEMETERY *(Optional - See instructions)*

30. EMAIL ADDRESS *(Optional - See instructions)*

SECTION III - CERTIFICATION AND SIGNATURE

CERTIFICATION: By signing below, I certify that I am the Claimant identified in item 23, or an individual signing for the Claimant identified in Item 34. All of the information entered on this form about the Claimant is true and correct to the best of my knowledge. A fraudulent statement that leads to burial in a national cemetery or receiving other benefits from the VA could result in disinterment from that national cemetery and other penalties in accordance with the law. I acknowledge that otherwise eligible individuals may be barred from burial for committing certain serious crimes, as provided under 38 U.S.C. § 2411. VA will therefore validate a previous determination of eligibility at the time of need to check for those bars in addition to law changes or Claimant status changes that may affect eligibility of the Claimant.

***31. YOUR SIGNATURE**

***32. DATE**

***33. YOUR RELATIONSHIP TO THE CLAIMANT IN ITEM 23** *(Check one; See instructions)*
☐ A. SELF *(Stop here. Leave Items 34-37 blank)*
☐ B. INDIVIDUAL SIGNING FOR THE CLAIMANT who is under 18 years of age, is mentally incompetent, or is physically unable to sign the pre-need application *(Complete items 34 through 37)*

***34. NAME OF INDIVIDUAL FROM ITEM 33B COMPLETING FOR THE CLAIMANT** *(Last, First, Middle Name)*

***35. MAILING ADDRESS OF INDIVIDUAL COMPLETING THIS FORM FOR THE CLAIMANT** *(Street, City, State, and Zip Code, P.O. Box, Rural Route, etc.)*

***36. TELEPHONE NUMBER** *(Include Area Code)*

37. EMAIL ADDRESS *(Optional)*

VA FORM
MAY 2017 **40-10007**

INSTRUCTIONS FOR COMPLETING VA FORM 40-10007 APPLICATION FOR PRE-NEED DETERMINATION OF ELIGIBILITY FOR BURIAL IN A VA NATIONAL CEMETERY

For more complete information on eligibility requirements for burial in a VA national cemetery, visit the National Cemetery Administration online at http://www.cem.va.gov/cem/burial_benefits/eligible.asp or call the National Cemetery Scheduling Office at 1-800-535-1117. For the purposes of this form, the term burial includes inurnment (above ground remains placement in a columbarium) and scattering of ashes, (if the cemetery chosen offers those options). **A Pre-Need determination of eligibility does not guarantee burial in a specific VA national cemetery. Burial in a specific VA national cemetery will be scheduled at the Time of Need.** In order to assist in completing this form, specific instructions and explanations for certain items are given below.

SECTION I: VETERAN/SERVICEMEMBER

Eligibility for burial in a VA national cemetery is based on the qualifying service of a Veteran/Servicemember. This section of the form is used to determine if qualifying service exists. Not all items are mandatory, however, answers to questions will aid VA in searching for records in archives to support the claim.

Item 13	**Military status used to apply for eligibility determination:** For VA benefit purposes, a Veteran is a person who served in the active military, naval, or air service, and who was discharged under conditions other than dishonorable. VA will determine on a case-by-case basis whether certain Reserve duty qualifies. If eligibility derives from a status not listed, or if the individual is not certain of the status, check "Other" and submit evidence of service and VA will provide appropriate assistance. Servicemembers who die on active duty are eligible for burial. If you are arranging burial for an active duty Servicemember or his or her dependents, you should contact a local funeral home or the National Cemetery Scheduling Office at 1-800-535-1117 to expedite processing.
Item 17	**Discharge - Character of Service:** Please indicate one type of "Discharge - Character of Service": Honorable; General; Entry Level Separation/Uncharacterized; Other Than Honorable; Bad Conduct; or Dishonorable. If uncertain of the type of discharge or character of service, indicate "Other" and include available supporting documents.
Item 22	**Supporting military service documents:** VA recommends that you attach photocopies of readily available supporting documents so that we can make the determination quickly. Documents may include the most recent discharge document (DD Form 214) showing the highest rank and valor awards and decorations, active duty service records other than for training purposes, or active duty for a minimum of 24 continuous months for enlisted Servicemembers after September 7, 1980; for officers, after October 16, 1981, or the full period for which the person was called to active duty. If you are unable to locate copies of military records, apply anyway, as VA will attempt to obtain records necessary to make a determination.

SECTION II: CLAIMANT INFORMATION

Item 23	**Each Claimant requires a separate VA Form 40-10007.**
	23b. Spouse means a person who is or was legally married to a Veteran. Surviving Spouse mean a person who was legally married to a Veteran at the time of the Veteran's death and includes a surviving spouse who had a subsequent remarriage. A non-Veteran spouse of a Veteran whose marriage to the Veteran was dissolved by divorce or annulment issued by an authoritative court is not eligible for burial in a VA national cemetery.
	23c. An unmarried adult child of the Veteran is an individual who became permanently physically or mentally disabled and incapable of self-support before reaching 21 years of age, *or* before reaching 23 years of age if pursuing a full-time course of instruction at an approved educational institution. If you are making a claim for an unmarried adult child, please provide supporting documentation such as recent medical documentation pertaining to the disability, date of onset of the disability, and the age of the child when diagnosed with this disability. VA recommends that you provide photocopies. Note: *Minor children of eligible Veterans are eligible for burial in a VA national cemetery. The minor child of an eligible Veteran is a child who is unmarried and who is under 21 years of age; or who is under 23 years of age and is pursuing a full-time course of instruction at an approved educational institution.*
	23d. Please explain your Claimant status or relationship to the Veteran/Servicemember.
Items 29 and 30	A list of VA national cemeteries is available online at http://www.cem.va.gov/cem/cems/allnational.asp **A favorable Pre-Need determination of eligibility does not guarantee burial in a specific national cemetery. Burial in a specific VA national cemetery will be scheduled at the time of need.** If you provide an email address, VA may use your email address to communicate with you about your claim and burial benefits.

SECTION III: CERTIFICATION AND SIGNATURE

Items 31 and 32	**The pre-need application must be signed (Item 31) and dated (Item 32) for VA to process.**
Item 33	You must indicate **your relationship to the claimant** in Item 33.
	33a. Check (A) if you are the claimant
	33b. Check (B) and complete Items 34-37 if your are signing for a claimant who has not attained the age of 18 years, is mentally incompetent, or is physically unable to sign the pre-need application. You may be a court-appointed representative, a person who is responsible for the care of the individual (including a spouse or other relative), or an attorney in fact or agent authorized to act on behalf of the claimant under a durable power or attorney. If the claimant is in the care of an institution, a manager or principal officer of the institution may sign the form. Please attach supporting documents or an affidavit establishing your position relative to the claimant.

Privacy Act Information: VA considers the responses you submit confidential (38 U.S.C. 5701). VA may only disclose this information outside the VA if the disclosure is authorized under the Privacy Act, including the routine uses identified in the VA system of records, 175VA41A, published in the Federal Register. VA considers the requested information relevant and necessary to determine maximum benefits under the law.

Respondent Burden: Public reporting burden for this collection of information is estimated to average 20 minutes per response, including the time to review instructions, search existing data sources, gather the necessary data, and complete and review the collection of information. The obligation to respond is voluntary and not required to obtain or retain benefits.

REVERSE OF VA FORM 40-10007, MAY 2017

GENERAL INFORMATION SHEET
CLAIM FOR STANDARD GOVERNMENT HEADSTONE OR MARKER

RESPONDENT BURDEN - Public reporting burden for this collection of information is estimated to average 15 minutes per response, including the time for reviewing instructions, searching existing data sources, gathering and maintaining the data needed, and completing and reviewing the collection of information. VA cannot conduct or sponsor a collection of information unless it has a valid OMB number. Your obligation to respond is voluntary, however, your response is required to obtain benefits. Send comments regarding this burden estimate or any other aspect of this collection of information, including suggestions for reducing this burden to the VA Clearance Officer (005R1B), 810 Vermont Avenue, NW, Washington, DC 20420. Please DO NOT send claims for benefits to this address.

BENEFIT PROVIDED

a. HEADSTONE OR MARKER

Only for Veterans who died on or after November 1, 1990 - Furnished for the grave of any eligible deceased Veteran. Will be provided for placement in private cemeteries regardless of whether or not the grave is already marked with a privately-purchased headstone or marker.

Only for Veterans who died before November 1, 1990 - Furnished for the **UNMARKED GRAVE** of any eligible deceased Veteran. The applicant must certify the grave is **unmarked. For Veterans that served prior to World War I, a grave is considered marked when a headstone/marker displays the decedent's name only, or if the name was historically documented in a related document, such as by a number that is inscribed on a grave block and is recorded in a burial ledger. For service during and after World War I, a grave is considered marked if a headstone/marker displays the decedent's name and date of birth and/or death, even though the Veteran's military data is not shown.**

b. MEMORIAL HEADSTONE OR MARKER - Furnished **for placement in a cemetery only** to commemorate a deceased eligible Veteran whose remains have not been recovered or identified, were buried at sea, donated to science, or cremated and the remains scattered. May not be used as a memento. Check box in block 28 and explain in block 27.

c. MEDALLION - Eligible Veterans may receive a Government-furnished headstone or marker, or a medallion, but not both. *If requesting a medallion, please use VA Form 40-1330M.*

WHO IS ELIGIBLE - Any deceased Veteran discharged under honorable conditions and any member of the Armed Forces of the United States who dies on active duty. A deceased Veteran discharged under conditions other than honorable may also be eligible. A copy of the deceased Veteran's discharge certificate (DD Form 214 or equivalent) or a copy of other official document(s) establishing qualifying military service must be attached. **Do not send original documents; they will not be returned. Service after September 7, 1980, must be for a minimum of 24 months continuous active duty or be completed under special circumstances, e.g., death on active duty.** Persons who have only limited active duty service for training while in the National Guard or Reserves are not eligible unless there are special circumstances, e.g., death while on active duty, or as a result of training. Reservists and National Guard members who, at time of death, were entitled to retired pay, or would have been entitled, but for being under the age of 60, are eligible; a copy of the Reserve Retirement Eligibility Benefits Letter must accompany the claim. Reservists called to active duty other than training and National Guard members who are Federalized and who serve for the period called are eligible. Service prior to World War I requires detailed documentation, e.g., muster rolls, extracts from State files, military or State organization where served, pension or land warrant, etc.

WHO CAN APPLY - Federal regulation defines "applicant" as the decedent's Next-of-Kin (NOK); a person authorized in writing by the NOK; or a personal representative authorized in writing by the decedent. Written authorization must be included with claim. A notarized statement is not required.

HOW TO SUBMIT A CLAIM

FAX claims and supporting documents to **1-800-455-7143.**
IMPORTANT: If faxing more than one claim - fax each claim package (claim plus supporting documents) individually, i.e., disconnect the call and redial for each submission.

MAIL claims to: **Memorial Programs Service (41B)**
Department of Veterans Affairs
5109 Russell Road
Quantico, VA 22134-3903

A Government headstone or marker may be furnished only upon receipt of a fully completed and signed claim with required supporting documentation.

SIGNATURES REQUIRED - The applicant signs in block 17; the person agreeing to accept delivery (consignee) in block 22, and the cemetery or other responsible official in block 24. If there is no official on duty at the cemetery, the signature of the person responsible for the property listed in block 21 is required. Entries of "None," "Not Applicable," or "NA" cannot be accepted. State Veterans' Cemeteries are not required to complete blocks 17, 18, 22 and 23.

ASSISTANCE NEEDED - If assistance is needed to complete this claim, contact the nearest VA Regional Office, national cemetery, or a local veterans' organization. No fee should be paid in connection with the preparation of this claim. Use block 27 for any clarification or other information you wish to provide. Should you have questions when filling out this form, you may contact our Applicant Assistance Unit toll free at: 1-800-697-6947, or via e-mail at mps.headstones@va.gov.

TRANSPORTATION AND DELIVERY OF MARKER - The headstone or marker is shipped without charge to the consignee designated in block 19 of the claim. **The delivery will not be made to a Post Office box.** The consignee should be a business with full delivery address and telephone number. If the consignee is not a business explain fully in block 27. For delivery to a Rural Route address, you must include a daytime telephone number including area code in block 20. If you fail to include the required address and telephone number information, we cannot deliver the marker. The Government is not responsible for costs to install the headstone or marker in private cemeteries.

CAUTION - To avoid delays in the production and delivery of the headstone or marker, please check carefully to be sure you have accurately furnished all required information before faxing or mailing the claim. If inaccurate information is furnished, it may result in an incorrectly inscribed headstone or marker. Headstones and markers furnished remain the property of the United States Government and may not be used for any purpose other than to be placed at an eligible individual's grave or in a memorial section within a cemetery.

DETACH AND RETAIN THIS GENERAL INFORMATION SHEET FOR YOUR RECORDS.

VA FORM
FEB 2014 **40-1330**   ALL PREVIOUS VERSIONS OF THIS FORM WILL BE OBSOLETE ON OCTOBER 1, 2014

ILLUSTRATIONS OF STANDARD GOVERNMENT HEADSTONES AND MARKERS

UPRIGHT HEADSTONE
WHITE MARBLE OR
LIGHT GRAY GRANITE

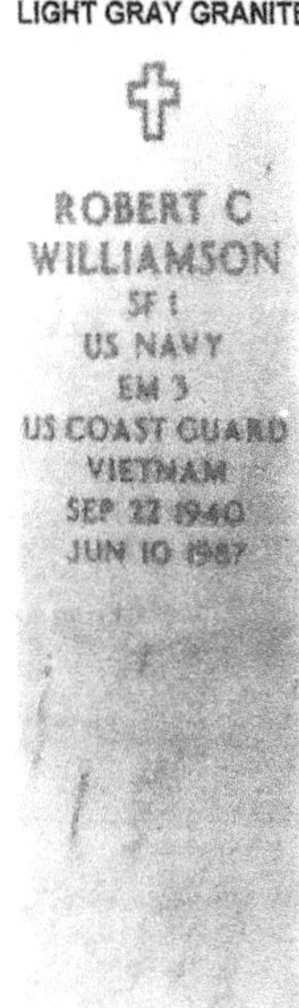

This headstone is 42 inches long, 13 inches wide and 4 inches thick. Weight is approximately 230 pounds. Variations may occur in stone color, and the marble may contain light to moderate veining.

BRONZE NICHE

This niche marker is 8-1/2 inches long, 5-1/2 inches wide, with 7/16 inch rise. Weight is approximately 3 pounds; mounting bolts and washers are furnished with the marker. Used for columbarium or mausoleum interment. Also provided to supplement a privately-purchased headstone or marker for eligible Veterans who died on or after November 1, 1990 and are buried in a private cemetery.

FLAT MARKERS
BRONZE

This grave marker is 24 inches long, 12 inches wide, with 3/4 inch rise. Weight is approximately 18 pounds. Anchor bolts, nuts and washers for fastening to a base are furnished with the marker. The base is not furnished by the Government.

LIGHT GRAY GRANITE OR WHITE MARBLE

This grave marker is 24 inches long, 12 inches wide, and 4 inches thick. Weight is approximately 130 pounds. Variations may occur in stone color; the marble may contain light to moderate veining.

NOTE: Civil War Era headstones - In addition to the headstone and markers pictured, two special styles of upright headstones are available for those who served with Union Forces during the Civil War or for those who served in the Spanish-American War, and another for those who served with the Confederate States of America during the Civil War. Requests for these special styles should be made in block 27 of the claim. It is necessary to submit detailed documentation that supports eligibility. Inscriptions on these headstone types are intentionally limited to assure historic accuracy. For example, only rank above 'Private' was historically authorized; emblems of belief and the words 'Civil War' are not provided.

INSCRIPTION INFORMATION

MEMORIAL HEADSTONES AND MARKERS (remains are not buried). The words "In Memory Of" are mandatory and precede the authorized inscription data. The words "In Memory Of" are only inscribed when remains are not available.

MANDATORY ITEMS of inscription at Government expense are: Legal Name, Branch of Service, Year of Birth, Year of Death, and for State Veterans and National Cemeteries only, the section and grave number. Branches of Service are: U.S. Army (USA), U.S. Navy (USN), U.S. Air Force (USAF), U.S. Marine Corps (USMC), U.S. Coast Guard (USCG), U.S. Army Air Forces (USAAF), and other parent organizations authorized for certain periods of time; and special units such as Women's Army Auxiliary Corps (WAAC), Women's Air Force Service Pilots (WASP), U.S. Public Health Service (USPHS), and National Oceanic & Atmospheric Administration (NOAA). Different examples of inscription formats are illustrated above. More than one branch of service is permitted, subject to space availability.

OPTIONAL ITEMS are identified on the claim in boxes with bold outlines. These items may be included at Government expense if desired. Optional items include month and day of birth in block 5A, month and day of death in block 5B, highest rank attained in block 7, awards in block 9, war service in block 10, and emblem of belief in block 12. War service includes active duty service during a recognized period of war and the individual does not have to serve in the actual place of war, e.g., Vietnam may be inscribed if the Veteran served during the Vietnam War period, even though the individual never served in the country. Supporting documentation must be included with the claim if you wish to include the highest rank and/or awards.

ADDITIONAL ITEMS may be inscribed at Government expense if they are requested on the initial claim and space is available. Examples of additional items include appropriate terms of endearment, nicknames (in expressions such as "OUR BELOVED POPPY"), military or civilian credentials or accomplishments such as DOCTOR, REVEREND, etc., and special unit designations such as WOMEN'S ARMY CORPS, ARMY AIR CORPS, ARMY NURSE CORPS or SEABEES. All requests for additional inscription items should be stated in block 27, and are subject to VA approval. No graphics, emblems or pictures are permitted except available emblems of belief, the Medal of Honor, and the Southern Cross of Honor for Civil War Confederates.

RESERVED SPACE for future inscriptions **at private expense**, such as spousal or dependent data, is allowed if requested in block 27 and if space is available. Only two lines of space may be reserved on flat markers due to space limitations. Reserved space is unnecessary on upright marble or granite headstones as the reverse side is available for future inscriptions.

INCOMPLETE OR INACCURATE INFORMATION ON THE CLAIM MAY RESULT IN ITS RETURN TO THE CLAIMANT, A DELAY IN RECEIPT OF THE HEADSTONE OR MARKER, OR AN INCORRECT INSCRIPTION.

Form approved, OMB No. 2900-0222
Expiration Date: Feb. 18, 2017
Respondent Burden: 15 minutes

Department of Veterans Affairs 1. FOR VA USE ONLY	**IMPORTANT:** Please read the General Information Sheet before completing this form. Type or print clearly all information except for signatures. Illegible printing could result in an incorrect headstone or marker or delivery. *Blocks outlined in bold are optional inscription items. Unless indicated otherwise* all other blocks **must** be completed. **MILITARY DISCHARGE DOCUMENTS OR RELATED SERVICE INFORMATION ARE REQUIRED.**

2. NAME OF DECEASED TO BE INSCRIBED ON HEADSTONE OR MARKER *(NO NICKNAMES OR TITLES PERMITTED)*

FIRST *(Or Initial)*   MIDDLE *(Or Initial)*   LAST   SUFFIX

3. GRAVE IS:
- ☐ CURRENTLY MARKED *(with privately purchased marker)*
- ☐ NOT MARKED

VETERAN'S SERVICE AND IDENTIFYING INFORMATION *(Use numbers only, e.g., 05-15-1941)*

4. VETERAN'S SOCIAL SECURITY NO. OR SERVICE NO.

SSN: OR SVC. NO.:

PERIODS OF ACTIVE MILITARY DUTY *(For additional space use Block 27)*

	6A. DATE(S) ENTERED			6B. DATE(S) SEPARATED		
	MONTH	DAY	YEAR	MONTH	DAY	YEAR

5A. DATE OF BIRTH			5B. DATE OF DEATH		
MONTH	DAY	YEAR	MONTH	DAY	YEAR

7. HIGHEST RANK ATTAINED *(No pay grades)*

8. BRANCH OF SERVICE *(Check applicable box(es) - must be consistent with rank in Box 7)*

ARMY	NAVY	MARINE CORPS	COAST GUARD	AIR FORCE	ARMY AIR FORCES	MERCHANT MARINE	OTHER *(Specify)*
☐	☐	☐	☐	☐	☐	☐	☐

9. VALOR OR PURPLE HEART AWARD(S) *(Documentation must be provided)*

MEDAL OF HONOR	DST SVC CROSS	NAVY CROSS	AIR FORCE CROSS	SILVER STAR	BRONZE STAR MEDAL	PURPLE HEART	OTHER *(Specify)*
☐	☐	☐	☐	☐	☐	☐	☐

10. WAR SERVICE *(Check applicable box(es))*

WORLD WAR II	KOREA	VIETNAM	PERSIAN GULF	OTHER *(Specify)*
☐	☐	☐	☐	☐

11. TYPE OF HEADSTONE OR MARKER REQUESTED *(Check one)*

FLAT BRONZE	FLAT GRANITE	UPRIGHT MARBLE	FLAT MARBLE	BRONZE NICHE	UPRIGHT GRANITE
☐ B	☐ G	☐ U	☐ F	☐ Z	☐ V

12. DESIRED EMBLEM OF BELIEF

EMBLEM NUMBER

☐ NONE   ☐ *(Specify) (See reverse side of this form for available emblems)* ___________

13A. NAME AND MAILING ADDRESS OF APPLICANT *(No., Street, City, State, and ZIP Code)*

13B. DAYTIME PHONE NO. OF APPLICANT

14. E-MAIL ADDRESS *(Optional)*

15. FAX NO. *(Optional)*

16. ARE YOU:
- ☐ NEXT OF KIN *(Specify relationship)* ___________
- ☐ AUTHORIZED REPRESENTATIVE ON BEHALF OF DECEDENT *(Include Written Authorization)*
- ☐ AUTHORIZED REPRESENTATIVE ON BEHALF OF NEXT OF KIN *(Include Written Authorization)*

CERTIFICATION: By signing below I certify the headstone or marker will be installed in the cemetery listed in block 21 at no expense to the Government and all information entered on this form is true and correct to the best of my knowledge. I also certify, to the best of my knowledge, that the decedent has never committed a serious crime, such as murder or other offense that could have resulted in imprisonment for life, has never been convicted of a serious crime, and has never been convicted of a sexual offense for which he or she was sentenced to a minimum of life imprisonment.

PENALTY: The law provides severe penalties, which include fine or imprisonment, or both, for the willful submission of any statement or evidence of a material fact, knowing it to be false or for the fraudulent acceptance of any benefit to which you are not entitled.

17. SIGNATURE OF APPLICANT	18. DATE *(MM/DD/YYYY)*

19. NAME AND DELIVERY ADDRESS OF BUSINESS (CONSIGNEE) THAT WILL ACCEPT PREPAID DELIVERY *(No., Street, City, State, and ZIP Code)*; **P.O. BOX IS NOT ACCEPTABLE**	20. DAYTIME PHONE NO. *(Include Area Code)*	21. NAME AND ADDRESS OF CEMETERY WHERE GRAVE IS LOCATED *(No., Street, City, State, and ZIP Code)*

CERTIFICATION: By signing below I agree to accept prepaid delivery of the headstone or marker.

22. PRINTED NAME AND SIGNATURE OF PERSON REPRESENTING BUSINESS (CONSIGNEE) NAMED IN BLOCK 19	23. DATE *(MM/DD/YYYY)*

CERTIFICATION: By signing below I certify the type of headstone or marker checked in block 11 is permitted in the cemetery named in block 21.

24. PRINTED NAME AND SIGNATURE OF CEMETERY OR OTHER RESPONSIBLE OFFICIAL	25. DAYTIME PHONE NO. *(Include Area Code)*	26. DATE *(MM/DD/YYYY)*

27. REMARKS *(Additional inscription space will vary in size according to the type of marker)*

28. CHECK BOX BELOW IF REMAINS ARE NOT BURIED AND EXPLAIN IN BLOCK 27 *(e.g., buried at sea, remains scattered, etc.)* ☐ REMAINS NOT BURIED	29. SECTION/GRAVE NO. *(State Cemetery Only)*

VA FORM FEB 2014 **40-1330**

CLAIM FOR STANDARD GOVERNMENT HEADSTONE OR MARKER

ALL PREVIOUS VERSIONS OF THIS FORM WILL BE OBSOLETE ON OCTOBER 1, 2014

AVAILABLE EMBLEMS *(See block 12)*

The graphics shown below are of 20 representative emblems of belief for placement on Government-furnished headstones/markers.

EMBLEMS OF BELIEF AVAILABLE:

LATIN CROSS (01)
BUDDHIST (Wheel of Righteousness) (02)
JUDAISM (Star of David) (03)
PRESBYTERIAN CROSS (04)
RUSSIAN ORTHODOX CROSS (05)
LUTHERAN CROSS (06)
EPISCOPAL CROSS (07)
UNITARIAN CHURCH (Flaming Chalice) (08)
UNITED METHODIST CHURCH (09)
AARONIC ORDER CHURCH (10)
MORMON (Angel Moroni) (11)
NATIVE AMERICAN CHURCH OF NORTH AMERICA (12)
SERBIAN ORTHODOX (13)
GREEK CROSS (14)
BAHAI (9 Pointed Star) (15)
ATHEIST (16)
MUSLIM (Crescent and Star) (17)
HINDU (18)
KONKO-KYO FAITH (19)
COMMUNITY OF CHRIST (20)
SUFISM REORIENTED (21)
TENRIKYO CHURCH (22)
SIECHO-NO-IE (23)
THE CHURCH OF WORLD MESSIANITY (Izunome) (24)
UNITED CHURCH OF RELIGIOUS SCIENCE (25)
CHRISTIAN REFORMED CHURCH (26)
UNITED MORAVIAN CHURCH (27)
ECKANKAR (28)
CHRISTIAN CHURCH (29)

CHRISTIAN & MISSIONARY ALLIANCE (30)
UNITED CHURCH OF CHRIST (31)
HUMANIST (AMERICAN HUMANIST ASSOCIATION) (32)
PRESBYTERIAN CHURCH (USA) (33)
IZUMO TAISHAKYO MISSION OF HAWAII (34)
SOKA GAKKAI INTERNATIONAL - USA (35)
SIKH (KHANDA) (36)
WICCAN (37)
LUTHERAN CHURCH MISSOURI SYNOD (38)
NEW APOSTOLIC CHURCH (39)
SEVENTH DAY ADVENTIST CHURCH (40)
CELTIC CROSS (41)
ARMENIAN CROSS (42)
FAROHAR (43)
MESSIANIC JEWISH (44)
KOHEN HANDS (45)
CATHOLIC CELTIC CROSS (46)
THE FIRST CHURCH OF CHRIST, SCIENTIST (Cross and Crown) (47)
MEDICINE WHEEL (48)
INFINITY (49)
LUTHER ROSE (51)
LANDING EAGLE (52)
FOUR DIRECTIONS (53)
CHURCH OF NAZARENE (54)
HAMMER OF THOR (55)
UNIFICATION CHURCH (56)
SANDHILL CRANE (57)
MUSLIM (Islamic 5 Pointed Star) (98)

To obtain the most recent information about headstones and markers including the complete and most current list of available emblems of belief (listing all names and graphics), please visit our website at www.cem.va.gov. You may also request a copy of this list by contacting our Applicant Assistance Unit toll free at 1-800-697-6947, or via e-mail at: mps.headstones@va.gov.

VA FORM 40-1330, FEB 2014

O. Chip Robinson

Department of Veterans Affairs — APPLICATION FOR UNITED STATES FLAG FOR BURIAL PURPOSES

PRIVACY ACT NOTICE: VA will not disclose information collected on this form to any source other than what has been authorized under the Privacy Act of 1974 or Title 38, Code of Federal Regulations 1.576 for routine uses (i.e., civil or criminal law enforcement, congressional communications, epidemiological or research studies, the collection of money owed to the United States, litigation in which the United States is a party or has an interest, the administration of VA programs and delivery of VA benefits, verification of identity and status, and personnel administration) as identified in the VA system of records, 58VA21/22/28, Compensation, Pension, Education, and Vocational Rehabilitation and Employment Records - VA, published in the Federal Register. Your obligation to respond is required to obtain or retain benefits. Giving us the veteran's SSN account information is voluntary. Refusal to provide the veteran's SSN by itself will not result in the denial of benefits. VA will not deny an individual benefits for refusing to provide his or her SSN unless the disclosure of the SSN is required by a Federal Statute of law in effect prior to January 1, 1975, and still in effect. The requested information is considered relevant and necessary to determine entitlement to benefits under the law. The responses you submit are considered confidential (38 U.S.C. 5701). Information submitted is subject to verification through computer matching programs with other agencies.

RESPONDENT BURDEN: We need this information to determine eligibility for issuance of a burial flag to a family member or friend of a deceased veteran (38 U.S.C. 2301). Title 38, United States Code, allows us to ask for this information. We estimate that you will need an average of 15 minutes to review the instructions, find the information, and complete this form. VA cannot conduct or sponsor a collection of information unless a valid OMB control number is displayed. You are not required to respond to a collection of information if this number is not displayed. Valid OMB control numbers can be located on the OMB Internet Page at www.reginfo.gov/public/do/PRAMain. If desired, you can call 1-800-827-1000 to get information on where to send comments or suggestions about this form.

IMPORTANT - Postmaster or other issuing official: Submit this form to the nearest VA regional office. Be sure to complete the stub at the bottom.

INFORMATION ABOUT THE DECEASED VETERAN *(Complete as much as possible)*
(Information provided is considered essential when applying for other VA benefits.)

1. FIRST, MIDDLE, LAST NAME OF VETERAN *(Print or type)*

2. MAIDEN NAME OR OTHER NAME(S) VETERAN USED WHILE ON ACTIVE DUTY *(Print or type)*

3. VA FILE NUMBER

4. SOCIAL SECURITY NUMBER

5. MILITARY SERVICE NUMBER/SERIAL NUMBER

6. BRANCH OF SERVICE *(Check box)*
[ ] ARMY [ ] NAVY [ ] AIR FORCE [ ] MARINE CORPS [ ] COAST GUARD [ ] SELECTED SERVICE [ ] OTHER *(Specify)*

7. DATE ENTERED ACTIVE DUTY *(or Selected Reserve)*

8. DATE RELEASED FROM ACTIVE DUTY *(or Selected Reserve)*

9. DATE OF BIRTH

10. DATE OF DEATH

11. DATE OF BURIAL

12. PLACE OF BURIAL *(Name of cemetery, city, and State)*

13. HAS DOCUMENTATION BEEN PRESENTED OR ATTACHED THAT SHOWS THE VETERAN MEETS THE ELIGIBILITY CRITERIA? *(See Paragraphs C, D, and E of the "Instructions")*
[ ] YES [ ] NO *(If "No," explain in Item 15, "Remarks" (See paragraph E of the "Instructions"))*

INFORMATION ABOUT THE FLAG RECIPIENT AND APPLICANT

14A. NAME OF PERSON ENTITLED TO RECEIVE FLAG

14B. RELATIONSHIP OF DECEASED VETERAN *(See Paragraph F of the "Instructions")*

14C. ADDRESS OF PERSON ENTITLED TO RECEIVE FLAG *(Number and street or rural route, city or P.O., State and ZIP Code)*

14D. TELEPHONE NUMBER

15. REMARKS

I **CERTIFY** that the statements made in this document are true and complete to the best of my knowledge. I further certify that the deceased veteran is eligible, in accordance with the attached instructions, for issue of a United States flag for burial purposes, and such flag has not been previously applied for or furnished.

16. SIGNATURE OF APPLICANT *(Sign in INK)*

17. ADDRESS OF APPLICANT *(Number and street or rural route, city or P.O., and ZIP Code)*

18. RELATIONSHIP TO DECEASED VETERAN

19. DATE SIGNED

PENALTY - The law provides that whoever makes any statement of a material fact knowing it to be false shall be punished by a fine, imprisonment, or both.

ACKNOWLEDGMENT OF RECEIPT OF FLAG (ONLY ONE FLAG MAY BE ISSUED FOR EACH DECEASED VETERAN)

20. SIGNATURE OF PERSON RECEIVING FLAG *(Sign in INK)*

21. DATE FLAG ISSUED

22. NAME AND ADDRESS OF POST OFFICE OR OTHER FLAG ISSUE POINT

FOR VA USE

DATE NOTIFICATION FORWARDED TO SUPPLY

STATION NUMBER

VA FORM 27-2008, MAR 2015 — SUPERSEDES VA FORM 27- 2008, JUL 2012, WHICH WILL NOT BE USED.

This stub is to be completed by the **POSTMASTER** or other issuing official. Upon receipt the VA Regional Office will detach and forward it to the appropriate Supply Officer.

NOTIFICATION OF ISSUANCE OF FLAG

DATE FLAG ISSUED

ISSUING POINT TELEPHONE NO.

ADDRESS OF POST OFFICE OR OTHER FLAG ISSUE POINT

SIGNATURE OF POSTMASTER OR OTHER ISSUING OFFICIAL

VA FORM MAR 2015 **27-2008** — SUPERSEDES VA FORM 27- 2008, JUL 2012, WHICH WILL NOT BE USED.

SEE INSTRUCTIONS

INSTRUCTIONS

A. How can I contact VA if I have questions?
If you have questions about this form, how to fill it out, or about benefits, contact your nearest VA regional office. You can locate the address of the nearest regional office in your telephone book blue pages under "United States Government, Veterans" or call 1-800-827-1000 (Hearing Impaired TDD line 1-800-829-4833). You may also contact VA by Internet at https://iris.va.gov/.

B. How do I apply for a burial flag?
Complete VA Form 27-2008, and submit it to a funeral director or a representative of the veteran or other organization having charge of the funeral arrangements or acting in the interest of the veteran. You may get a flag at any VA regional office or U.S. Post Office. When burial is in a national, State or military post cemetery, a burial flag will be provided.

C. Who is eligible for a burial flag?
Generally, veterans with an other than dishonorable discharge. *Note:* This includes veterans who served in the Philippine military forces while such forces were in the service of the U.S. armed forces under the President's Order of July 26, 1941 and died on or after April 25, 1951, and veterans who served in the Philippine military services are eligible for burial in a national cemetery.

Veterans who were entitled to retired pay for service in the reserves, or would have been entitled to such pay but not for being under 60 years of age.

Members or former members of the Selected Reserve (Army, Air Force, Coast Guard, Marine Corps, or Naval Reserve; Air National Guard; or Army National Guard) who served at least one enlistment or, in the case of an officer, the period of initial obligation, or were discharged for disability incurred or aggravated in line of duty, or died while a member of the Selected Reserve.

D. Who is not eligible for a burial flag?
Veterans who received a dishonorable discharge.

Members of the Selected Reserve whose last discharge from service was under conditions less favorable than honorable.

Peacetime veterans who were discharged before June 27, 1950 and did not serve at least one complete enlistment or incur or aggravate a disability in the line of duty.

Veterans who were convicted of a Federal capital crime and sentenced to death or life imprisonment, or were convicted of a State capital crime and sentenced to death or life imprisonment without parole, or were found to have committed a Federal or State capital crime but were not convicted by reason of not being available for trial due to death or flight to avoid prosecution.

Discharged or rejected draftees, or members of the National Guard, who reported to camp in answer to the President's call for World War I service but who, when medically examined, were not finally accepted for military service.

D. Who is not eligible for a burial flag? *(Continued)*
Persons who were discharged from World War I service prior to November 12, 1918, on their own application or solicitation by reason of being an alien, or any veterans discharged for alienage during a period of hostilities.

Persons who served with any of the forces allied with the United States in any war, even though United States citizens, if they did not serve with the United States armed forces.

Persons inducted for training and service who, before entering such training and service were transferred to the Enlisted Reserve Corps and given a furlough.

Former temporary members of the United States Coast Guard Reserve.

E. What documentation is required in order to receive a burial flag?
Provide a copy of the veteran's discharge documents that shows service dates and the character of service, such as DD Form 214, or verification of service from the veteran's service department or VA. Various information requested, is considered essential to the proper processing of the application. Ensure these areas are completed as fully as possible. *Note:* If the claimant is unable to provide documentary proof, a flag may be issued when a statement is made by a person of established character and reputation that he/she personally knows the deceased to have been a veteran who meets the eligibility criteria.

F. Who is eligible to receive a burial flag?
Only one flag may be issued for each deceased veteran. Generally, the flag is given to the next-of-kin as a keepsake after its use during the funeral service. The flag is given to the following person(s) in the order of precedence listed:

surviving spouse

children, according to age

parents, including adoptive, stepparents, and foster parents

brothers or sisters, including brothers or sisters of half blood

uncles or aunts

nephews or nieces

others, such as cousins or grandparents

When there is no next-of-kin, VA will furnish the flag to a friend making a request for it. If there is no living relative or one cannot be located, and no friend requests the flag, it must be returned to the nearest VA facility.

Note: The flag cannot be replaced if it is lost, destroyed, or stolen. Additionally, a flag may not be issued after burial unless it was impossible to obtain a flag in time to drape the casket or accompany the urn before burial. If the next-of-kin or friend is requesting the flag after the veteran's burial, he or she must personally sign the application and explain in Item 15 "Remarks" the reason that prevented timely application for a burial flag.

ISSUING OFFICIAL WILL DETACH THIS SHEET AND PRESENT IT TO THE RECIPIENT OF THE FLAG

USE OF THE FLAG

1. This flag is issued on behalf of the Department of Veterans Affairs to honor the memory of one who has served our country.

2. When used to drape the casket, the flag should be placed as follows:

(a) Closed Casket - When the flag is used to drape a closed casket, it should be so placed that the union (blue field) is at the head and over the left shoulder of the deceased.

(b) Half Couch (Open) - When the flag is used to drape a half-couch casket, it should be placed in three layers to cover the closed half of the casket in such a manner that the blue field will be the top fold, next to the open portion of the casket on the deceased's left.

(c) Full Couch (Open) - When the flag is used to drape a full-couch casket, it should be folded in a triangular shape and placed in the center part of the head panel of the casket cap, just above the left shoulder of the deceased.

3. During a military commitment ceremony, the flag which was used to drape the casket is held waist high over the grave by the pallbearers and, immediately after the sounding of "Taps," is folded in accordance with the illustration below.

4. Folding the flag (see illustration below):

5. The flag should not be lowered into the grave or allowed to touch the ground. When taken from the casket, it should be folded as shown (see illustration).

6. The flag should form a distinctive feature of the ceremony of the unveiling of a statue or monument, but it should never be used as a covering for the statue or monument.

7. The flag should never be fastened, displayed, used, or stowed in such a manner as will permit it to be easily torn, soiled, or damaged in any way.

8. The flag should never have placed upon it, nor any part of it, nor attached to it, any mark, insignia, letter, word, figure, design, picture, or drawing of any nature.

9. The flag should never be used as a receptacle for receiving, holding, carrying, or delivering anything.

10. The flag, when badly worn, torn, or soiled should no longer be publicly displayed, but privately destroyed by burning in such a manner as to convey no suggestion of disrespect or irreverence.

CORRECT METHOD OF FOLDING THE UNITED STATES FLAG

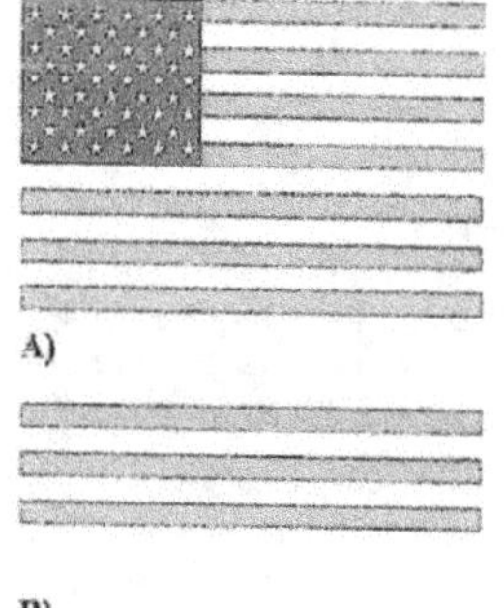

A)

(A) Straighten out the flag to full length and fold lengthwise once, folding the lower striped section of the flag over the blue field.

B)

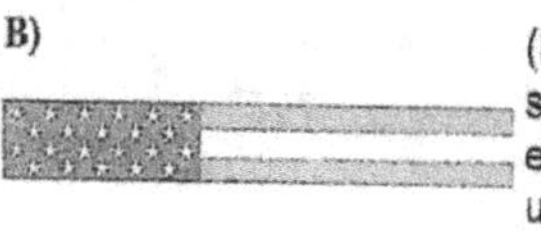

(B) Fold the flag lengthwise a second time to meet the open edge, making sure that the union of stars on the blue field remains outward in full view.

C)

(C) A triangular fold is then started by bringing the striped corner of the folded edge to the open edge.

D)

(D) The outer point is then turned inward, parallel with the open edge to form a second triangle.

E)

(E) The diagonal or triangular folding is continued toward the blue union until the end is reached, with only the blue showing and the form being that of a cocked (three corner) hat.

Social Security Administration	TOE 120/145/155	Form Approved OMB No. 0960-0013

APPLICATION FOR LUMP-SUM DEATH PAYMENT*

I apply for all insurance benefits for which I am eligible under Title II (Federal Old-Age, Survivors, and Disability Insurance) of the Social Security Act, as presently amended, on the named deceased's Social Security record.

(This application must be filed within 2 years after the date of death of the wage earner or self-employed person.)

* This may also be considered an application for insurance benefits payable under the Railroad Retirement Act.

1.	(a) PRINT name of Deceased Wage Earner or Self-Employed Person (herein referred to as the "deceased")	FIRST NAME, MIDDLE INITIAL, LAST NAME		
	(b) Check (X) one for the deceased		☐ Male	☐ Female
	(c) Enter deceased's Social Security Number			
2.	PRINT your name	FIRST NAME, MIDDLE INITIAL, LAST NAME		
3.	Enter date of birth of deceased *(Month, day, year)*			
4.	(a) Enter date of death *(Month, day, year)*			
	(b) Enter place of death *(City and State)*			
5.	(a) Did the deceased ever file an application for Social Security benefits, a period of disability under Social Security, supplemental security income, or hospital or medical insurance under Medicare?	☐ Yes *(If "Yes," answer (b) and (c).)*	☐ No ☐ Unknown *(If "No" or "Unknown," go on to item 6.)*	
	(b) Enter name(s) of person(s) on whose Social Security record(s) other application was filed.	FIRST NAME, MIDDLE INITIAL, LAST NAME		
	(c) Enter Social Security Number(s) of person(s) named in (b). (If unknown, so indicate)			
6.	ANSWER ITEM 6 **ONLY** IF THE DECEASED WORKED WITHIN THE PAST 2 YEARS.			
	(a) About how much did the deceased earn from employment and self-employment during the year of death?	AMOUNT $		
	(b) About how much did the deceased earn the year before death?	AMOUNT $		
7.	ANSWER ITEM 7 **ONLY** IF THE DECEASED DIED PRIOR TO AGE 66 AND WITHIN THE PAST 4 MONTHS.			
	(a) Was the deceased unable to work because of illness, injuries or conditions at the time of death?	☐ Yes *(If "Yes," answer (b).)*	☐ No *(If "No," go on to item 8.)*	
	(b) Enter the date the deceased became unable to work *(Month, day, year)*			
8.	(a) Was the deceased in the active military or naval service (including Reserve or National Guard active duty or active duty for training) after September 7, 1939 and before 1968?	☐ Yes *(If "Yes," answer (b) and (c).)*	☐ No *(If "No," go on to item 9.)*	
	(b) Enter dates of service.	From: *(Month, Year)*	To: *(Month, Year)*	
	(c) Has anyone (including the deceased) received, or does anyone expect to receive, a benefit from any other Federal agency?	☐ Yes	☐ No	
9.	Did the deceased work in the railroad industry for 7 years or more?	☐ Yes	☐ No	

Form **SSA-8** (11-2013) EF (11-2013)   Page 1

10.	(a) Did the deceased ever engage in work that was covered under the social security system of a country other than the United States?		☐ Yes *(If "Yes," answer (b).)*	☐ No *(If "No," go on to item 11.)*
	(b) If "Yes," list the country(ies).			

11.	(a) Is the deceased survived by a spouse? If "Yes", enter information about the marriage in effect at the time of death below. If "No", go on to item 11(b) if the deceased had prior marraiges or item 12 if the deceased never married.		☐ Yes	☐ No
	Spouse's Name *(including Maiden Name)*	When *(Month, day, year)*	Where *(Name of City and State)*	
	How marriage ended	When *(Month, day, year)*	Where *(Name of City and State)*	
	Marriage performed by: ☐ Clergyman or public official ☐ Other *(Explain in "Remarks")*	Spouse's date of birth (or age)	Spouse's Social Security Number *(If none or unknown, so indicate)* __ __ __ / __ __ / __ __ __ __	

(b) If the deceased had a prior marriage(s) that lasted at least 10 years, enter the information below. If the deceased married the same individual multiple times and the remarriage took place within the year immediately following the year of the divorce, and the combined period of marriage totaled 10 years or more, include the marriage. If none or unknown, so indicate.

Spouse's Name *(including Maiden Name)*	When *(Month, day, year)*	Where *(Name of City and State)*
How marriage ended	When *(Month, day, year)*	Where *(Name of City and State)*
Marriage performed by: ☐ Clergyman or public official ☐ Other *(Explain in Remarks)*	Spouse's date of birth (or age)	If spouse deceased, give date of death

Spouse's Social Security Number *(If none or unknown, so indicate)* __ __ __ / __ __ / __ __ __ __

(c) If the deceased has surviving children as defined in item 12 and he or she was married to the child's mother or father but the marriage ended in divorce, enter information on the marriage if not already listed in 11(b).. If none or unknown, so indicate.

Spouse's Name *(including Maiden Name)*	When *(Month, day, year)*	Where *(Name of City and State)*
How marriage ended	When *(Month, day, year)*	Where *(Name of City and State)*
Marriage performed by: ☐ Clergyman or public official ☐ Other *(Explain in Remarks)*	Spouse's date of birth (or age)	If spouse deceased, give date of death

Spouse's Social Security Number *(If none or unknown, so indicate)* __ __ __ / __ __ / __ __ __ __

12.	The deceased's surviving children (including natural children, adopted children, and stepchildren) or dependent grandchildren (including stepgrandchildren) may be eligible for benefits based on the earnings record of the deceased.

List below ALL such children who are now or were in the past 12 months UNMARRIED and:
- UNDER AGE 18   • AGE 18 TO 19 AND ATTENDING SECONDARY SCHOOL
- DISABLED OR HANDICAPPED (age 18 or over and disability began before age 22)

(If none, write "None.")

Full Name of Child	Full Name of Child

13.	Is there a surviving parent (or parents) of the deceased who was receiving support from the deceased either at the time the deceased became disabled under the Social Security law or at the time of death?	☐ Yes ☐ No *(If "Yes," enter the name and address of the parent(s) in "Remarks".)*
14.	Have you filed for any Social Security benefits on the deceased's earnings record before?	☐ Yes ☐ No

NOTE: If there is a surviving spouse, continue with item 15. If not, skip items 15 through 18.

15.	If you are not the surviving spouse, enter the surviving spouse's name and address here

110

16.	(a) Were the deceased and the surviving spouse living together at the same address when the deceased died?	☐ Yes (If "Yes," go on to item 17.)	☐ No (If "No," answer (b).)

(b) If either the deceased or surviving spouse was away from home (whether or not temporarily) when the deceased died, give the following:

Who was away?	☐ Deceased	☐ Surviving spouse	

Date last home	Reason absence began	Reason they were apart at time of death

If separated because of illness, enter nature of illness or disabling condition.

If you are the surviving spouse, and if you are under age 66, answer 17.

17.	(a) Are you so disabled that you cannot work or was there some period during the last 14 months when you were so disabled that you could not work?	☐ Yes ☐ No
	(b) If "Yes," enter the date you became disabled.	*(Month, day, year)*

Answer 18 ONLY if you are the surviving spouse.

18.	Were you married before your marriage to the deceased? If yes, enter information about your prior marriage(s) that lasted at least 10 years or ended due to death of the spouse. If you divorced then remarried the same individual within the year immediately following the year of the divorce and the combined period of marriage totaled at least 10 years, include the marriage. If you need more space, use "Remarks" section on back page or attach a separate sheet.	☐ Yes ☐ No

Spouse's name *(including maiden name)*	When *(Month, day, year)*	Where *(Name of City and State)*
How marriage ended	When *(Month, day, year)*	Where *(Name of City and State)*
Marriage performed by: ☐ Clergyman or public official ☐ Other *(Explain in Remarks)*	Spouse's date of birth (or age)	If spouse deceased, give date of death

Spouse's Social Security Number *(If none or unknown, so indicate)*   ___ ___ ___ / ___ ___ / ___ ___ ___ ___

For additional information about survivor benefits see our publication at www.socialsecurity.gov.

Remarks: *(You may use this space for any explanation. If you need more space, attach a separate sheet.)*

____

____

____

____

I declare under penalty of perjury that I have examined all the information on this form, and on any accompanying statements or forms, and it is true and correct to the best of my knowledge.

SIGNATURE OF APPLICANT	Date *(Month, day, year)*
Signature *(First name, middle initial, last name) (Write in ink)* ▶	Telephone Number(s) at Which You May Be Contacted During the Day (Area Code)

Mailing Address *(Number and street, Apt. No., P.O. Box, or Rural Route)*

City and State	ZIP Code	Enter Name of County (if any) in which you now live

Witnesses are required ONLY if this application has been signed by mark (X) above. If signed by mark (X), two witnesses to the signing who know the applicant must sign below, giving their full addresses.

1. Signature of Witness	2. Signature of Witness
Address (Number and street, City, State, and ZIP Code)	Address (Number and street, City, State, and ZIP Code)

112

Form **SSA-8** (11-2013) EF (11-2013)   Page 3

About the Author

O. Chip Robinson has been a freelance writer and journalist for nearly 40 years. She started her writing career at the early age of 16 with her first full-length manuscript, a historical fiction romance novel she titled "Everlasting Love". 

Unfortunately, that novel never made it to print, but she did not let that discourage her. She continued her love of writing and soon found that she preferred to write nonfiction, especially newspaper articles and human-interest stories.

Throughout her writing career, Chip has had many articles published in various newspapers, magazines, and blogs across the United States and abroad. Additionally, she has had several non-fiction and self-help books published geared toward helping everyday people prepare for the most important moments of their lives.

These days Chip spends time traveling, relaxing with her husband of 40 years, her loyal dogs, a Siberian Husky-Lab mix Magi Moo and Luci Boo, a Black Lab mix.

www.ingramcontent.com/pod-product-compliance
Lightning Source LLC
Chambersburg PA
CBHW080937120726
48003CB00011B/3193